I0170070

THE MOTHER TERESA EFFECT

TITLES BY ALICIA YOUNG

The Mother Teresa Effect:
What I Learned Volunteering for a Saint
(2016)

Two Eggs, Two Kids:
An Egg Donor's Account of Friendship, Infertility & Secrets
(2015)

The Savvy Bride's Guide:
Simple Ways to a Stylish & Graceful Wedding
(2015, 2014)

The Savvy Bride's Guide: Your Wedding Checklist
(2015, 2014)

The Savvy Girl's Guide to Grace:
Small Touches with Big Impact—at Home, Work & in Love
(2013)

THE
MOTHER TERESA
EFFECT

WHAT I LEARNED
VOLUNTEERING FOR A SAINT

ALICIA YOUNG

PARASOL PRESS LLC, TEXAS

Copyright © 2016 Alicia Young

All rights reserved. No portion of this book may be reproduced electronically, mechanically or by any other means without the express written permission of the publisher, except for the purposes of review.

Young, Alicia, author.
The Mother Teresa effect : what I learned
volunteering for a saint / Alicia Young.
pages cm
Includes bibliographical references and index.
LCCN 2016910019
ISBN 978-0-9965388-1-7 (pbk.)
ISBN 978-0-9965388-2-4 (ebook)

1. Young, Alicia—Diaries. 2. Volunteers—India—
Kolkata—Biography. 3. Voluntarism—India—Kolkata—
Case studies. 4. Teresa, Mother, 1910–1997—Influence.
5. Convents—India—Kolkata. 6. Spiritual formation.
7. Autobiographies. 8. Diaries. I. Title.

HN690.Z9V649 2016   361.3'7092
QBI16-900009

PARASOL PRESS LLC
PO Box 980456, Houston, TX 77098-0456
motherteresaeffect.net • aliciayoung.net

Book design by Monroe Street Studios
Author photo by Elizabeth Shrier. © 2014 Alicia Young

Printed in the United States of America
First printing 2016
10 9 8 7 6 5 4 3 2 1

FOR CHARMAINE, A CHILD OF CALCUTTA,

whose warmth, humor, and spirituality resonate

CONTENTS

INTRODUCTION 9

MOTHER TERESA: HER LIFE IN BRIEF 15

PART I: Getting Settled 17

PART II: Kalighat, the Home for the Dying 33

PART III: (Mother Teresa's Last) Christmas and New Year 55

PART IV: The Leprosy Ward 93

PART V: Back Home 127

"FIND YOUR OWN CALCUTTA" 137

THINKING OF TRAVELING TO INDIA? 139

ACKNOWLEDGMENTS 141

SELECT BIBLIOGRAPHY 144

ABOUT THE AUTHOR 147

THE 12 STAMPS PROJECT 150

DONATIONS 151

INDEX 152

INTRODUCTION

⮜⮞

I T'S A SEARING HOT DAY IN eighth-grade religion class, and the air conditioning is straining to make its presence felt.

Sister Paula is talking, but my mind is drifting to summer vacation and boy bands. I snap back to attention when she mentions Mother Teresa. My family is from Calcutta (now Kolkata), and we've always followed news of her. The teacher is quoting a story from Mother Teresa's 1979 Nobel Prize Lecture:

> *Some time ago in Calcutta we had great difficulty in getting sugar, and I don't know how the word got around to the children [but] a little boy of four years old, [a] Hindu boy, went home and told his parents: I will not eat sugar for three days, I will give my sugar to Mother Teresa for her children.*
>
> *After three days his father and mother brought him to our home. I had never met them before, and this little one could scarcely pronounce my name, but he knew exactly what he had come to do. He knew that he wanted to share his love.*
>
> MOTHER TERESA, MC
> © THE NOBEL FOUNDATION

This piques my interest. A four-year-old hears about the sugar shortage and decides to go without so that he can help others.

It isn't complicated.

It isn't grand.
It isn't long term.
But he does it. At age four.
Inspired by a woman he'd never met.
That's *The Mother Teresa Effect.*

⤐⟞

I grew up in a typical Catholic family in Perth, Australia. We're Anglo-Indian, meaning half British and half Indian. My father served on the parish council and also as an acolyte (a layperson who assists the priest, including giving Holy Communion). I recall him volunteering with a family friend, Astor, at the Saint Vincent de Paul Center. They would help deliver refrigerators, furniture, and clothing to longtime locals and recent migrants alike. My mother journeyed to Lourdes.

The Youngs occupied the last pew of the little makeshift church at Majella Primary School. Tables would be pushed aside and seating rearranged from classroom format to pews. One of my earliest memories of church is helping to collect copies of the *Hesed,* the parish newsletter, which lay scattered after Mass. In third and fourth grades, I took my turn doing liturgical movements, mortifying choreographed dances set to hymns during the service. Photos show us with long hair flowing, our A-line tunics festooned in swirling patterns of black, white, and purple. We looked like we'd escaped from a cult.

My older sisters went to the church youth group; my brother was an altar boy. In our late teens, my sister and I would saunter into Sunday Mass at the last minute, weary from a night of clubbing (eighteen is the entry age in Australia). First Communions and Confirmations punctuated the year, and later, engagements, weddings, and Baptisms as the family grew up and beyond the boundaries of our hometown.

When I was about eleven, my Auntie Grace visited from India; she was my father's only sister and a nun. We had black-and-white photos of her in an old-fashioned habit, complete with a stiff wimple (veil) similar to the one worn by Whoopi Goldberg in *Sister Act.* I recall thinking that when we met, she was so much warmer and more animated than I had expected from the photo. Her small stature and soft manner of speaking belied her inner strength.

My parents believed in the power of a simple gesture. Whenever we visited my grandfather in a nursing home, they would make a point of chatting to the other men in his room who rarely had company, offering chocolates or perhaps a newspaper. I have no doubt these small but significant acts planted seeds in us all. I would later see these actions echo in the volunteers in India.

As I look back, my parents also had a healthy attitude toward death. When our grandmother died, they bundled us off to the funeral, while others felt we were too young. Death was not something to be shied away from or imbued with fear. I recall a time when my husband, Jon, and I had not been dating long, and we stopped by my parents' home. My mother remarked they had reviewed their wills that day and I was to inherit her car. "Great!" I said. "Mine is having trouble with the starter. So if you could kick the bucket in the next few weeks . . ." We both laughed—but Jon was horrified and must have wondered what sort of ghoul he'd met.

⤜⤚

My parents had the first seven of their nine children in Calcutta, not too far from Motherhouse, the headquarters of the Missionaries of Charity. They followed Mother Teresa's life with interest. This continued even after moving the family to Australia (its wide, clean roads made a lasting impression), and they encouraged us to volunteer for the order.

I found the right time at age twenty-eight, from December 1996 through February 1997. At the time, Jon and I had been married less than three years and were living at a boarding school in Perth. We were residential staff to sixty teenage boys while studying and working part-time.

It was a Saturday morning, and we were surrounded by coffee and various sections of the newspaper when I spotted a feature article on Mother Teresa. Something clicked; I turned to Jon and said, "I need to work for her. Soon." Jon glanced up, saw my expression, and said simply, "Okay. We'll make it happen."

We were both navigating new careers. Jon had been a high school teacher, but returned to college to study geophysics; by then, he was working on his master's degree. I had been a social worker (mainly in child protection and mental health settings) and had gone back to school to study broadcast journalism. I would be finishing the course in November, about four months away; I could go to Calcutta straight after that. Once the job hunt got underway, I'd feel compelled to stay in town. Jon was scheduled to attend a conference in November in the US; I'd join him there and then together we'd head to India. He could stay for almost a week.

⚶

I wrote to Mother Teresa and was shocked when she wrote back personally. I had expected some sort of photocopied, general-issue response. Penned on small, quaint notepaper were two or three lines, thanking me for my interest and inviting me to join the volunteers. The note ended, "God bless you, M. Teresa, MC" (the latter initials referring to her order, the Missionaries of Charity). Unfortunately, this letter has been lost to the intervening twenty years and eight countries in which I've lived. I imagine—*hope*—it will turn up one day in the most unlikely place.

Jon wasn't raised in a religious family, and as time drew near, he became a little worried that I'd go to India and come back a nun. It didn't occur to him that they might not rush to sign up an outspoken, concert-loving, one-time go-go dancer with a navel ring. His concern made his unwavering support of the trip all the more loving and selfless.

The family was very supportive, and my parents took comfort in the fact I'd be based either with relatives (the first week) or in convents during my stay.

I read that Calcutta had almost a glut of volunteers, given so many people wanted to work for the Missionaries of Charity. Mindful of this, I decide to split my time with another location. I would stay at a rural hospital near the town of Siliguri, about forty miles from the tea plantations of Darjeeling, where I'd be based in the leprosy ward. I chose leprosy because the accompanying stigma made it every bit a social burden as a physical disease.

I have no medical training. My intention was to help with simpler tasks such as bathing and feeding the patients, to free up the volunteer nurses and doctors for more pressing work. Of course, many volunteers stayed far longer than I did. Some, such as an American woman called Tess, was there with her husband for a year or two. Her countryman, a doctor by the name of Harry, was there when I arrived in 1996 and planned to stay until the year 2000.

What you're about to read comes from my journal, as well as my letters to friends and family. The dates of some events are approximate, based on references in dated letters and cards. Except for my Auntie Grace, all other names have been changed. You'll see I extend my diary entries a little past my time in India, to share how the trip washed over me in ways big and small.

Sprinkled among the entries you'll find little boxes titled *The Mother Teresa Effect*. They feature thoughts from people of different cultures, backgrounds, and faiths (or no faith) who share the way Mother Teresa inspired them. Her influence has had a ripple effect through every country, tax bracket, and worldview, from the deeply philosophical to the wonderfully pragmatic.

The city I was based in has since reverted to its precolonial name of Kolkata; I retain "Calcutta" here to reflect the time in which the entries were written.

Mother Teresa was European, and many volunteers to India are foreigners. That said, we can't lose sight of the army of Indians who work tirelessly for their own people. They run nonprofits, raising both funds and awareness. They establish schools and lobby for social policies that better serve the poor. They volunteer, donate, and lend their skills and time to serve others.

We've all heard the cliché of the Westerner traveling east seeking enlightenment, and, likewise, the cliché of those in the developing world who need rescuing. Both stereotypes do a disservice. Please also keep in mind, while my volunteer experience no doubt shares common ground with others who were or are in India, no single account is definitive.

I felt propelled to go simply because I had so much; it was time to give back. In fact, I gained much more: lessons on compassion and grace, and insights into nonjudgment. And as presumptuous as it might first sound, the sisters showed us that we're often as busy as we choose to be. Yes, we might be occupied with children, aging parents, or a demanding boss, but somewhere, momentarily, there is room each day to decide how we spend our time.

If you'd like to see photos of my time in India, please visit my website at motherteresaeffect.net.

———//———

MOTHER TERESA
Her Life in Brief

MOTHER TERESA WAS BORN Gonxha (pronounced "GON-cha") Agnes Bojaxhiu ("boy-AR-choo") on August 26, 1910, in Skopje, present-day Macedonia. For someone so famous, surprisingly little is recorded about her early life. We know that Gonxha's parents, Nikola and Dranafile ("Drana" for short), were Albanian. Her father is variously described as a modest grocer, a prominent businessman, an importer, and a contractor in the construction industry. Whatever his livelihood, biographers agree he was a political activist, fighting for Albanian independence. Her mother was a homemaker. The Bojaxhius were devout Catholics, and the parish calendar provided a framework to faith and family life. Gonxha was the youngest of three; she had an older brother and sister.

When Gonxha was eight years old, her father died; speculation swirled that he was poisoned at the hands of political adversaries. Her mother took in sewing and embroidery to make ends meet, eventually opening a small fabric business. It was her mother's activities outside work, however, that perhaps had the most impact on her children. Drana was a compassionate woman and welcomed their poorer neighbors to eat with the family.

At age eighteen, Gonxha headed to Ireland to became a novice with the Sisters of Loreto. After professing her first vows in 1931, she took the name Sister Mary Teresa after Saint Thérèse of Lisieux (known as "the little flower"). She traveled to Darjeeling, India, for her last year of instruction, professing her final vows in 1937. From that point on, according to the Vatican, she was known as Mother Teresa. She taught for seventeen years in Calcutta and became fluent in Hindi and Bengali. Throughout, the plight of the poor had a deep impact on her.

In September 1946, Mother Teresa was traveling by train from Calcutta to Darjeeling; some say it was for an annual spiritual retreat, while others suggest she was sent to the country to recuperate after a bout of malaria. In any case, on that journey she received what she would refer to as "a call within a call." She said she heard the voice of God telling her to focus on the poor.

In 1950, the Vatican granted permission for her to begin a new order, the Missionaries of Charity. Sisters took the traditional vows of obedience, chastity, and poverty; Mother Teresa added a crucial fourth pledge, of dedication to the poorest of the poor. After working out of some rooms at a private home, in 1952 she opened Kalighat ("CAR-lee-gut"), the Home for the Dying Destitute. As such, it is referred to as "Mother's First Love." At the time of her death in 1997 at age eighty-seven, Mother Teresa's order spanned 123 countries, with 4,500 religious sisters carrying out her mission.

⸎

Saint Thérèse of Lisieux was born in September 1897; the future Saint Teresa died in September 1997. In the century that bookended their lives on earth, the world received a gift that still resonates today.

——⫶——

PART I
Getting Settled

ARRIVING IN INDIA

❦

Late November 1996

Jon and I arrive in Calcutta from the US, where he'd delivered his first academic paper at an earth-science conference.

My aunt Rita (known simply as Rita) picks us up with her driver in stifling heat and humidity. A ride of "technically forty-five minutes" to her apartment bloats past two hours, as the traffic inches along at a murderous rate. Calcutta is a city of twelve million people, and it seems as though every one of them is on the road right now. Horns blare impatiently and achieve nothing. Beggars encircle the car, leaning against it, their fingers poking through the sliver of an open window. We jostle around inside, our jet lag casting a dreamlike haze over it all. Hands thrust huge bouquets of roses against the glass; Rita nonchalantly explains they've likely been swiped from Christian graveyards (Hindus are cremated). The glacial pace of driving offers glimpses of street life: people rummaging through trash, cows weaving on and off the street, pollution enveloping it all.

My arm is still tender from my final hepatitis B shot. I'd begun the series of injections in Australia, and packed the needle and vial in my hand luggage. Yesterday we stopped at a US travel clinic for my final dose (I couldn't bring myself to do it, and Jon seemed a little too keen to try.) They wanted two hundred dollars for the two-minute job—make that a two-minute *jab*—and a ream of paperwork. Instead, we got to the airport and asked to see the doctor on call. She was an Indian lady, and when she learned our destination, she graciously administered the shot at no charge.

❦

We finally arrive at Rita's home. Jon and I will have almost a week here together before he heads back to Australia. Rita's apartment is spacious and well appointed, decorated with understated elegance. The family has domestic staff (a way of life for a quarter-billion Indians), and they're still referred to here as servants. Hospitality is taken seriously and offered graciously.

We're each brought a refreshing glass of *nimbu pani*, a mixture of water, a squeeze of lemon juice, and a dash of honey. It's touted as a healthy, gentle way to cleanse the system.

The air is fragrant with hand-ground *masalas* (spices). A platter of *samosas* appears, delicious triangles of golden puff pastry filled with a medley of onions, potatoes, and peas. (Rita's staff eat the same dishes prepared for the family. This is not the norm.)

The longtime cook cheerfully needles Jon to eat five times more than anyone else; she considers it her duty to fill his six-foot-five frame. We smile, accustomed to being lovingly badgered to eat; relatives at home are mortified if we visit and fail to consume half our body weight. Next door is a large pond, handy to walk around. At the rate we're eating, we'll need it. "Watch how Indians walk," Rita counsels. "They almost glide along." And it's true; it's as though minimal effort is exerted in the heat.

The pace inside is relaxed, in stark contrast to the bustle on the street. There is no reliance on fast food or something frozen thrown into the microwave. Each dish is cooked from scratch and presented beautifully. And just as meals are planned ahead, so are other rituals. The hot water system, known as a "geezer," must be turned on at least thirty minutes before it's needed to ensure a steamy supply. There is no option to hop in for a quick shower on the spur of the moment or before you dash out the door.

Our gifts of liquor, chocolates, and other items are stored in a locked cupboard.

The staff is quietly horrified that I wear minimal jewelry. They fret discreetly to Rita that every woman, no matter how poor, should adorn her neck, wrists, and fingers, if only with colored string. That I would choose to go out with a simple wedding band and watch mystifies them.

There is a knock at the door. Rita had given out new clothes to workers around the apartment complex a month or two before, to celebrate Diwali (the Festival of Light). A man politely requests his as he'd been out of town.

A few days later, the jet lag is subsiding.

I've been looking forward to visiting Auntie Grace at the convent where she lives. She has been a nun for more than sixty years and is now in her mid-eighties. Her memory is razor sharp, and she affectionately chides me for not having replied promptly when she wrote to me at age fourteen, more than a decade earlier. I'll be moving into this convent when Jon leaves. Most volunteers to Calcutta stay in the budget hotels on Sudder Street; my experience will offer a different way of life, and I'm eager to sample it.

Auntie Grace is not a sister with the Missionaries of Charity but belongs to a different Catholic order. She worked with Mother Teresa for decades on many of the same committees and recalls that while her famous colleague had a good sense of humor, she could be very strident. Grace remembers a time Teresa turned to her during a meeting and announced, "I'm sending you another forty orphans next month." "Mother, we can't feed the ones we have," Grace countered. "God will provide," responded Teresa, and that was that. She was already checking it off her agenda.

Grace recalls that when the Missionaries of Charity was first established, the sisters existed on very little. They would be sent to the market with instructions to bring home only enough food for that day. Having no money, they then would stare at the floor with their baskets beside them, arms crossed in humility. And there, they would wait in silence for someone to offer to pay on their behalf. This could take minutes, hours, or most of the day.

By the time we provide all the family updates, Grace is looking tired, so we say our goodbyes.

We head next to Kalighat, where I'll be based. We're both curious to see it, and Jon will feel better about my absence if he can picture the environment.

Kalighat goes by several names. Formally, it is Nirmal Hriday, the Missionaries of Charity's Home for the Dying Destitute. It also translates to Home of the Pure Heart. "Kalighat" derives from "Kali," the name of a Hindu goddess, and "ghat," the word for the mouth of a river, such as the nearby Hooghly River.

A sister graciously makes time for us. She explains that when Mother Teresa founded the Missionaries of Charity in 1950, she began scouring locations for a home. Despite teaching in India for seventeen years, she was initially greeted with curiosity and skepticism. Some days, this would escalate to outright hostility, as people suspected her real agenda was to convert people to Christianity. Thus, she found it difficult to secure a base. Legend holds that in time, she learned of a Hindu priest dying of cholera; she nursed him when others, fearful of catching the disease, would not. In gratitude, the community worked with local officials to give her a building off the main Hindu temple, formerly a dormitory for out-of-town worshippers. This is where I'll volunteer.

⊶

By evening, we transition to another world as we head to a wedding with Rita. Wedding season (roughly between October and December) is in full swing as it brims with auspicious dates to marry. In a country approaching a population of one billion, wedding season is so big that it has a direct impact on the global gold market. Nor is it fueled only by demand for rings, but all manner of gold bangles, bracelets, and neck-laces. While 18-carat gold is popular in the West, here 22-carat gold is strongly favored.

Marriage ceremonies in the middle and upper classes of India are multiday affairs of lavish feasts and intricate services. We arrive on the third day to join a throng of more than a thousand people. The groom arrives on a white horse, which is draped in garlands of fresh flowers and shiny beads; sometimes an elephant is the ride of choice. He is sur-rounded by a procession of well-wishers, singing and dancing, who have accompanied him from his home.

Guests line up to congratulate the couple, who sit on magnificent thrones. The bride is resplendent in red, the wedding color in India (white, while traditional in the West, is the color of death here). Her hands and feet are covered in *mendhi*, temporary henna tattoos applied in intricate designs, often with her groom's initials woven in discreetly as a romantic tribute.

Once we greet them, we follow the crowd to another area where everyone is fed generously. There is no silverware, yet people eat with finesse, elegantly rolling their food into bite-size balls with the tips of their fingers. The tables are dotted with bowls of lemon water for rinsing. Usually, no meat or alcohol is served.

As with any wedding, guests are decked out in their finest clothes. Bright shades are favored, and the crowd is awash in jewel colors. Amid the happy chatter, we meet women called Pinkie, Twinkie, Cookie, and Dimple, their childlike nicknames in carefree contrast to their sophistication and elegance. In the background, there is another dynamic at play. I notice multiple camera crews, documenting not only the happy couple but also their guests. Photographers snap photos of young women of marriageable age. "Oh, those," waves off one society matron; "they photograph all the potential brides. Then future mothers-in-law check them out later and do research on the family." My relatives are considered progressive as they will entertain the idea of a respectable "love match" found by their adult children, as long as the family presents well.*

The festive evening ends on a more somber note: Jon and I are up all night with fragile stomachs. The food tonight was delicious, but our systems need time to adjust.

THE MOTHER TERESA EFFECT

Mother Teresa of Calcutta exemplifies Christianity's great tradition and practice of compassion.   HIS HOLINESS, THE DALAI LAMA

I saw a cartoon where the boy had x-ray vision. Mother Teresa was like that. She saw right into someone's heart, even if they were smelly and dirty.   GABRIEL, AGE 8, DALLAS

---

* I write in more detail about wedding traditions in India and many other cultures in my books *The Savvy Bride's Guide: Simple Ways to a Stylish & Graceful Wedding* and *The Savvy Bride's Guide: Your Wedding Checklist.*

CALCUTTA: FIRST IMPRESSIONS

CALCUTTA. THERE IS NO denying the sense and scale of crowding. Every available space we can see, whether on the road, the pavement, or a store shelf, is claimed and brimming. There is no break in the visual assault, nowhere for your eyes to pause a moment, resting on a blank wall or a clear patch of dirt. If the scene were a drawing, each inch of the page would be teeming with imagery, sketches within sketches.

Babies and children wear heavy black kohl eyeliner, or else a "third eye" painted on their foreheads, to ward off evil spirits. Many have their noses pierced, while their bare feet are caked with dirt and calloused beyond their years. Private schoolchildren weave among them on foot or in rickshaws, in crisp uniforms of pristine white shirts and quaint hats.

Men wear shorts as they bathe in the alleyways, drawing on buckets of soapy water and rinsing off with jugs held above their heads. They are neither ostentatious nor embarrassed; it is everyday life. The air is thick with pollution. Children play with trash and scour the debris for anything they can eat, sell, or use. Other youngsters shout in glee as they take turns spinning a tire down the road with a stick.

The ground is bright red with globs of scarlet-colored saliva, caused by chewing the popular betel nut; it also stains the gums bright red and lends some people a comical, vampire-like appearance. Pots and pans are washed on the sidewalk, the water used and reused. Windows have no fly screens; shutters open to let in the sun and (not quite fresh) air. Feral dogs roam through it all. Laundry flutters on makeshift clotheslines, sheets and underwear on display for the entire street. The sheer density of people intensifies everything, whether enchanting or stomach-churning.

The streets are a battleground of vehicles competing for road space, and drivers brandish their horns like weapons. A ceaseless round of aggressive buzzing, insistent beeping, and timid tooting pierces the day. Buses and trams (streetcars) are packed to overflowing. Elbows and limbs fly in every direction; occasionally, so do tempers.

On the whole, though, Indians seem remarkably easygoing despite the crush of people that engulfs them. Picture a school bus crammed with 120 people—and the odd goat on its way to be sacrificed at a nearby temple. People hang off the sides of the bus, blasé as they risk life and limb to oncoming traffic. Ticket collectors make a clicking sound right in your face as they ask for fare. Depending on your route, you might hear a continual soundtrack of *Kidderpore! Kidderpore!*, *Ballygunge! Ballygunge!*, or *Howra! Howra!* Imagine reciting these destinations twenty times a minute—with marbles in your mouth—and you'll get a sense of their clarity.

Tuk-Tuks (rickshaws, powered by either small motors or reed-thin legs) are everywhere, threadbare but robust. I spot one with a battered wooden carriage and tires that are depressingly thin. A shade cloth hangs tattered yet resolute. The driver's seat is a piece of scrap metal, and I wonder how the rickshaw *walla*'s back feels at the end of the day. Mopeds weave in and out of this mayhem, often carrying a family of three. There are no helmets to be seen. Colorful saris, the traditional women's clothing in India, flutter in the wind. I recall my parents saying there are no driving lanes in Calcutta; you have to drive through to create one. This is true; drivers stay on the left—except when they don't.

Rubbish is discarded on the street, dumped into ponds, and flung out of cars, seemingly without a second thought.

The pollution is fine, infuriating, and all-encompassing. Dirt invades every pore. Clothes, furniture, and bottles become filthy, enveloped in a thin layer of dust. The water is hard, and my hair is beginning to resemble straw. Café workers replenish "bottled" water at the tap and quickly reseal it. I remind myself to never drink tap water (at least not wittingly), eat fresh salads, or order a drink with ice.

Throughout all this, billboards command attention. It seems that every third ad touts skin-fading creams, complete with a pale Bollywood actress beckoning you to try some.

Then there are the moving billboards: the truck art that emblazons so many vehicles. From hefty cargo road-trains to small, zippy delivery vans, transport is bedecked in painstaking illustrations. Their sheer colors are what draw you first; they're ablaze in bright hues. The green and saffron orange of the Indian flag are popular choices. Gods or goddesses are often depicted at the front of the vehicle, sometimes with fresh flowers tied to the grill beneath them (which wilt within minutes, choked by fumes or heat). Elsewhere, the fierce face of a demon warns would-be thieves to think twice before breaking in.

People urinate on the side of the road at will. Choose any strip of sidewalk at random, and you'll likely find a home, a public urinal, and a place of business. Crows are everywhere—and they seem oversized to me.

Amid it all, there is tremendous beauty and nobility. The crumbling architecture still stands proud. The former grandeur evokes a different time, an unhurried time, with its intricate moldings and artistic features so carefully crafted. And the people carry themselves with quiet dignity. Smiling comes as naturally as breathing, even amid such squalor.

I wonder when the *real* culture shock will set in—and how. Everything we've seen, heard, and smelled so far is starkly new and mesmerizing. Still, I'm yet to register an inner seismic shift in the way I've read and heard about. Perhaps it's yet to come. Perhaps it will wash over me more gradually. Perhaps it won't really hit me until I'm back home, sitting in a café and reading the paper. I'm no global traveler, so I can only imagine that hearing stories of Calcutta while growing up has insulated me. That, and the family "slide-show nights" (fascinating as children) and "home-movie nights" (excruciating as teenagers) that we'd gather to watch.

∞

Tears flow as I say goodbye to Jon. We've been married three years, together six, and we've never spent so much time apart. We plan to write a river of letters and to call once a week.

THE MOTHER TERESA EFFECT

Nonjudgment. Okay, less *judgment.* ANGELA, TORONTO

I volunteered at Motherhouse during summer holidays from the Loreto boarding school in Asansol. I started as an eleven-year-old in 1969 and kept going till 1971, dividing my time between Motherhouse and the Little Sisters of the Poor. I used to help feed the older people, or assist in changing their linen or making beds.

I met Mother Teresa three times. The first two occasions were a brief greeting, when my dad would pick me up and they would chat like old friends. The final time, I was talking to an elderly lady who was bedridden. I was telling her about my dad being sick and also having to stay in bed. Mother came up to me and she said, "I know of the trials your father is facing. My sisters and I remember your family in our prayers daily. God will decide and provide. You must be strong." Then she patted me on the head and moved away. The following year, my dad died and my mom got a beautiful letter from Mother Teresa.

I'll always remember how calm and gentle she was, soft-spoken, not a real touchy-feely type. She would look directly at you when she was speaking to you, as though you were the only person there. And she loved patting people, on the head, shoulder, or arm, just a brief point of contact. JOSEPHINE, PERTH

REGISTERING AT MOTHERHOUSE

Monday, December 2, 1996
54A AJC Bose Road, Calcutta, West Bengal, India 700016

There are addresses famous the world over: 1600 Pennsylvania Avenue, for example, or 10 Downing Street. A markedly modest building in Calcutta attracts the same curiosity and is arguably more revered. It's Motherhouse, the headquarters of the Missionaries of Charity.*

I've come here to register as a volunteer. It's very humid, with the sticky air sparking rivulets of sweat down my neck. The four-story facade is disintegrating yet stately, nestled in a neighborhood with shops strung in colorful garlands, on a road of blaring horns and pedestrians weaving through traffic. Motherhouse is built around a small open-air courtyard. There is a grotto of the Virgin Mary with tiered plants and flowers arranged around her in salute.

I follow the cheerful noise inside; the building is crammed with volunteers from around the world. The air is thick with accents, joyful in tone but jarring in volume. A few people wave small flags from home to more easily find their compatriots; it's only natural to gravitate to your own. The volunteers come in every shape, size, age, and ethnicity, and they will fan out from this central point to the various houses run by the Missionaries of Charity. There are many individuals like me, but also couples, small clusters, and large groups, whether school- or faith-based. I meet Sister Priscilla, who oversees the registration of volunteers. She possesses a lovely inner calm, and I imagine her in the eye of a hurricane, unhurried and unstressed.†

We're asked to list our preferences on where we'll be located. The Missionaries of Charity run eight or nine homes in Calcutta, covering every

---

* Today the building is even more popular, as visitors pay their respects at Mother Teresa's tomb.

† She would later be short-listed to replace Mother Teresa.

age group and many circumstances. Nirmala Shishu Bhavan (or simply Shishu Bhavan), for example, is for newborn babies to children aged ten. I'd be happy to help on occasion, but it's best I don't base myself there. I'd want to scoop them all up and take them home, so I wouldn't be much help. Other houses serve the disabled and mentally ill, both children and adults. An orphanage for street children operates a few tram stops away.

But I am drawn to Kalighat, the Home for the Dying Destitute. Given the sparse lives of the street people, the opportunity to provide someone even a trace of comfort in their dying days is compelling. And, of course, death is the great unifier. Despite the uncertainties and dramatic disparities of our lives, none of us escape it.

Mother Teresa is unwell and not seeing many people, but an excited gush announces her appearance in one part of Motherhouse.

THE MOTHER TERESA EFFECT

Can a receptionist evoke Mother Teresa? Ours does. Our school is in a severely economically depressed area. The parents are janitors, street vendors, cleaning ladies; many are illiterate. They come in, often shy and lacking assertion. Our receptionist treats them with respect and dignity. They arrive cap-in-hand and walk out tall.

PRINCIPAL S., MEXICO CITY

Mother Teresa took care of people that others wouldn't.

DANIEL, AGE 9, PERTH

MOVING INTO THE CONVENT

Tuesday, December 3, 1996

I'm excited to get settled into the convent where Auntie Grace lives and to start volunteering. I'm up early and packed while the rest of the household is still sleeping. The morning drags on, and when everyone wakes, they seem to be moving on IST (Indian Standard Time, aka slow motion).

The convent is a two-story building tucked into a quiet enclave on a main road; walking through its gates offers an immediate respite from the hurtling trucks, beeping taxis, and "auto-rics" (motorized rickshaws). I sense it will be a welcome threshold at the end of a workday. Simple but colorful gardens dot the landscape and lend an air of cheer.

I meet with the Sister Superior, who is inviting and warm. She begins to give me an overview of their routine, then laughs and dismisses it all with a gentle wave of her hand: I'll learn as I go along.

I leave my bags in a front room as I set off to find Auntie Grace. I am delighted to be in the same building (housing a mix of retired nuns and female residents), and I look forward to evening chats after work.

My room is located on the second floor and embraces austerity. There is a simple bed, bureau, and desk. A few feet beyond that is a shower stall with no shower curtain, or shower, for that matter. Instead, the concrete area and drain has an area for two buckets (for hot and cold water), a footstool for bathing, and an indoor clothesline. A toilet and small basin complete the washroom.

Painted green shutters extend halfway up the window, finished with a filmy curtain so thin I can easily make out the people outside. I won't need an alarm clock—if the sun doesn't get me up, the bells will, summoning us all to morning Mass.

The floor is concrete, and the bed, apparently designed for munchkins, has a short iron frame. I tell myself I'm simply too tall. Hmmm. This, from the girl who would fill out waitressing applications as *Height:*

5'6" (and scrawl next to it *5'9" with tall hair*). I have a small taste of what Jon feels, folding his towering frame into regular beds.

I love my room.

I'm surrounded by mostly elderly female boarders, a mix of Anglo-Indian (half British, half Indian) widows and single women, almost all of whom grew up under British rule. They are lovely people, and gracious. An orange appears at my door (which extends only partway up the wall), then some sweet curd (thick yogurt), and later, a pencil. It's a heartwarming welcome, especially given my neighbors are of relatively modest means. Each gift involves a lengthy visit and a list of questions.

By the time I unpack, we're called to lunch. I meet more of the sisters in the dining area. They welcome me kindly, and I feel grateful to be here.

There is egg curry and rice (which makes me smile; growing up in Australia, we knew the paycheck was being stretched whenever this curry dish appeared); side dishes of sliced onions, tomatoes, and cucumbers are a welcome way to cool my tongue. We round off the meal with fruit, which today is pomegranates. The sisters explain it is known as "the fruit of patience." The pith is finicky and comes away only in small, stubborn pieces. It can't be rushed, but the process is meditative . . . or so I'm told.

Everyone helps clear the table. As we wash, dry, and stack dishes, I feel as though I've landed at an adult summer camp. The atmosphere is upbeat and chatty.

❧

Back in my room late in the afternoon, I start to bathe just as another welcome wagon calls. I'm advised not to bathe at night, as the washroom light will attract mosquitoes, and everyone is wary of malaria.

Jon calls tonight, still a bit jet-lagged after his return home. It is wonderful to hear his voice, but unfortunately the call comes at the worst time. The Sister Superior is leading prayers before the meal when the phone starts ringing loudly and insistently down the hall. Finally, someone goes to answer it, and I feel like a naughty schoolgirl as I slip out to talk to him.

Last week, I was a tourist. If Calcutta is a sea of humanity, as it's often described, I'm about to dip my toe in as a volunteer.

THE MOTHER TERESA EFFECT

I'm no longer embarrassed to ask for a doggie bag in a restaurant. I don't want to waste food when I consider how many people in my city, my country, and around the world will go to bed hungry tonight.

BETH, MELBOURNE

She did so much with so little; it made me look closer at the charities we pledged to. We've retained one and released one, replacing it with a nonprofit which directs 92 percent of funds raised to its cause.

S. AND T., TALLAHASSEE

I went to the same covent school in Dublin where, decades before, Mother Teresa had trained as a novice. She visited when I was fourteen, and we were all hugely excited. I remember her standing at the top of some steps and waving. I had to strain my neck to see the top of her bowed head; I was struck by how tiny she was. It also seemed poetic that someone so small in stature could command such respect and adoration.

Fast forward a few years, and I visited Mauritius when I was eighteen. Part of my trip was spent at Mother Teresa's Center for the Homeless (or unwanted). It was hard to believe it existed on this island paradise. It certainly wasn't the side of town they put on tourist brochures! I cannot look back at the place with rose-tinted glasses; it was grim and, at times, frightening. Some of the people were so wretched, many of them badly disabled, physically and mentally. I spent only a couple of days there before deciding to finish my volunteer work at a refuge for battered women. Yes, indeed, that was a breeze in comparison to the Mother Teresa Center! The truth is, I felt unable to deal with the hardships faced by the poor people in that first home. How the nuns coped was truly amazing. I was humbled by their compassion, and I still am today. CIARA, LONDON

———— // ————

PART II
Kalighat, the Home for the Dying

MY FIRST DAY

Wednesday, December 4, 1996

The bells start pealing before 5:00 A.M. in the predawn darkness, and while I toss and turn, they ensure I make it to Mass on time. Given my aunt is a nun here, it wouldn't do to be late.

I'd packed reasonably old clothes to wear. Today I put on jeans and a light, long-sleeved T-shirt—no bare midriffs! I'm traveling with some religious brothers for a few days until I get the hang of the public transport; I meet them at the convent gate. The trams are crowded, and people hang off the sides as it snakes its way around, inhaling and exhaling commuters. The brothers show me the right stop, and I enjoy the short walk to the building. I am mindful of my surroundings and stride with purpose; this also helps the vendors to bypass me as they hawk their wares.

I step in from the bright morning sun to the cool and comparative darkness of Kalighat's entry area. There are two wards, each smaller than a two-bedroom apartment. One ward houses roughly fifty men, the other, fifty women, mostly former street people. The nuns tell us that prior to coming here, they might have worked but fallen sick and then endured hard times. Others might have been pavement dwellers, one of several generations living together on the sidewalk; they likely spent most days begging for scraps of food or some coins with which to feed their children. A few men and women find Kalighat on their own, or they are brought in by relatives, no longer able to provide care themselves. Most, however, have been collected by the religious brothers, sisters, and volunteers, often from the shanty areas surrounding the nearby Howra train station.

They arrive in various states of ill health, from weeping sores and broken bones to malaria and tuberculosis. Some have open wounds teeming with maggots or insects. Others have broken bones that have set in deformed ways due to a complete lack of medical care. Whatever their condition, it is made worse by a common denominator of malnourishment and dehydration. Their immune systems are shredded, their eyes haunted. If lice are suspected, their heads are shaved and beards clipped off. Their clothes, usually threadbare, tattered, and soiled, are discarded immediately and replaced with a clean set.

Patients rest on narrow cot beds, about a foot off a polished concrete floor. They are arranged in rows sufficiently spaced to allow someone to walk between them, and a painted number is stenciled near each bed. The sisters know all the patients by name, but in busy times, these numbered beds are handy. I sense a flashback to the shorthand used during my waitressing days. "Bed 14!" someone calls out, rather than "Table 14!" It helps cut through the language and time barriers. Sisters and volunteers commingle, buzzing around their charges. A simple chalkboard keeps tracks of admissions, discharges, and deaths each day.

Many patients weigh sixty pounds or less, more akin to the images of starving African children we grew up seeing on ads for World Vision or UNICEF. Some are considerably frailer than that, their skeletal bodies ravaged by life on the street. Some have lost chunks of flesh, as though someone took an ice-cream scoop roughly to their thigh or calf.

I am immediately drawn to the spiritual honesty of Kalighat. The nuns here speak about the gift of a "good death," a final gesture equally significant to bestow on a stranger as on a loved one. For some patients, it is a home for the destitute to recuperate from the aftereffects of life on the street; they do recover and eventually leave. Ultimately, though, Kalighat is a hospice, a final stop where one can die in dignity and comfort, tendered to with compassion. A sister quotes Mother Teresa, deeply touched by a man who confided, "I have lived as an animal on the street, but I am going to die like an angel."

The novices (those training to be nuns), sisters, and Missionaries of Charity Brothers wear solid-blue aprons. The men are known as the MC Brothers for short; I think they sound like a hip-hop band.

The volunteers are known by their blue and white checkered pinafores. Novices stand out by their plain white saris, not having yet earned the blue stripes of those who pledge their final vows of religious life. (The cloth for these famous garments is woven by leprosy patients living on the fringes of Calcutta, at the Missionaries of Charity's home in Titagarh.)

Kitchen workers squat or sit, preparing vegetables for lunch and dinner directly on the concrete floor. They use semicircular blades to slice and dice. It's a colorful corner of the Home, with mounds of green beans, red onions, potatoes ("always potatoes," sighs one volunteer), and rice in abundance. Two large sinks are beside them, built into the floor.

We serve the patients breakfast in tin bowls. There is cereal, with watered-down powdered milk or tea to moisten the kernels of popped rice. A boiled egg nestles in one corner, and occasionally a wedge of fruit. Some can feed themselves, others need help.

The patients call the volunteers either "auntie" or "uncle." It's both amusing and a little disconcerting to be addressed this way by women fifty years my senior.

Tea is steeped in battered metal teapots. Staff or volunteers craft a giant tea bag from a hollowed-out *brinjal* (eggplant) and then stuff it with tea leaves. It's very resourceful and creative, but it infuses the beverage with a dreadful aftertaste, especially as the vegetable begins to break down in the steaming liquid. Everyone gags on it initially, I'm told. By day three, they say, you'll barely notice it. I doubt it, but I smile and say nothing.

When everyone is fed, we clean the plates with a paste of detergent and ash from the coal fires, which apparently has antibacterial properties. Technology has no place at Kalighat. There are no industrial dishwashers; simplicity and people power drive the routine. Mother Teresa values minimalism and feels it's crucial for the sisters and volunteers to better relate to our patients.

We take a brief break, and the volunteers gather on the rooftop for tea. We nibble square, flat cookies dubbed "UN biscuits," as they're apparently the same type the United Nations hands out in war zones. They taste like cardboard, but are packed with nutrients. Of course, it's gracious that snacks are provided at all. A volunteer laments that she came to India at the wrong time for mangoes. The summer mango season is especially popular. The patients relish its luscious orange flesh, sucking on the large seeds to extract every bit of juice.

After our break, we bathe and dress the men and women who call Kalighat home. They know the drill and surrender with a smile. Some can walk on their own; a few crawl along the floor, their limbs withered but their independence shining through. Others need assistance. Our patients are so thin, it's not a strain to pick them up and carry them to be bathed. The first is Bhakti. I run the water in the dim light and hand her soap, mindful of her privacy if she has the strength to wash herself. But she is tired, so I try to be gentle as her skin seems as delicate as crepe paper. As I towel-dry her, I can't help but note her complete lack of padding; her bones protrude all over. We work together to get her dressed. I want to make conversation, if only to make her more comfortable, but I don't speak Bengali. In any case, she likely sees someone different every day. I'm yet another anonymous face. We make do with pointing, smiling, and nodding. I carry her back and get her settled. The pattern is set.

I arrive back at the convent, a little tired but mostly invigorated. The atmosphere is encouraging, and the camaraderie sustaining.

THE MOTHER TERESA EFFECT

I was snowed under with work deadlines when not one but three *young people asked me to write letters supporting their college applications. My gut was to decline, but I looked up to my bookshelf and saw a picture of Mother Teresa. She planted seeds; so could I.*

HANK, NEW ORLEANS

We did a class on empathy for the elderly. We put on glasses with smeared lenses to make it harder to see. We put pebbles in our shoes and walked around. We wore earplugs to cut out sound around us. Mother Teresa talked about compassion. She'd totally get it.

AVA, BERKELEY

FRUSTRATION YIELDS TO REFLECTION

❧

Thursday, December 5, 1996

After Mass at the convent, it's a breakfast of various curries. I grew up on mild Indian fare and associate it with family, childhood, and comfort food. Still, spices this early in the morning take an adjustment. I'm grateful for the sisters' hospitality, but I slip in a prayer for something bland. I recall my cousin munching on raw chilies at age seven, and my eyes water at the thought. I might be Anglo-Indian, but somehow I bypassed the spicy-food gene. If I had to imagine my last meal, I'd be torn between mild chicken curry or a lamb roast with all the trimmings.

I'm disappointed that I have to take a break from Kalighat one day after starting; volunteers usually have Thursdays off. Instead, I take the opportunity to meet more women at the convent.

It feels presumptuous to knock on people's doors, so I let a few residents know that I'm offering foot massage, and the word spreads from there. It gives us a chance to chat alone or in small groups.

Late in the afternoon, I head to the post office counter. I buy a bundle of forty aerograms, pages of loose-leaf international mail designed to be folded like an envelope. The paper tears if you look at it harshly, and the gum along the edges is dry and doesn't stick. The woman checks and rechecks that I want forty. She flashes her hands four times. I nod. She writes down the number. I nod. She shows me the stack. I nod. When she delays yet again, I cock my head to the side and raise an eyebrow. "Acha," she says and finally sells them to me, but not before calling over her friend in the next store and regaling her with the entire skit.

Acha ("UTCH-ar") seems to me the most flexible word in Bengali. It is used interchangeably through countless conversations to signal approval, permission, awe, or simple resignation. You might moan, "I've had a bad day," and someone will murmur a sympathetic "acha." On the other hand, you might proclaim in wide-eyed wonder, "Did you hear? Grandad used to be a lion tamer!"—and they will tsk-tsk with a clicked tongue and offer an "acha" in shared shock. It punctuates everything.

On the stroll back to the convent, I notice many stores along the main road where phone calls can be made and faxes can be sent and received. The employees balk when they see the writing I have crammed on the page, but a few extra rupees settle it. They will also deliver any incoming faxes to the convent for twenty cents.

THE MOTHER TERESA EFFECT

My twin sister and I got almost two thousand dollars in graduation money. We donated half to a local women's shelter. The manager was shocked; that felt good.   A.J. AND ROB, MODESTO

My mother answered a knock at the door and was startled when a neighbor asked if she could spare any underwear. As it happened, she did have a new packet and gave it freely. Someone else might have laughed or raised an eyebrow. She gracefully and simply complied, preserving the woman's dignity in what must have been a difficult request.   TAMMY, PERTH

Friday, December 6, 1996

The ceiling fans at Kalighat whir above us optimistically, but their blades never seem to cut a swath through the heavy, muggy air. The windows in the women's ward are small and high on the wall. At least the men's room has markedly bigger, better windows to let the light stream in.

It reminds me of a story I heard from a news cameraman when I interned at a local TV station. British journalist Malcolm Muggeridge visited Mother Teresa in 1970. Though he approached the assignment in the skeptical, formal mode of an investigative reporter, an experience at Kalighat left an imprint the rest of his life. The crew needed to record inside the Home, but the cameraman protested it was too dark. Yet, when the film was processed, it came out beautiful and bright. There seemed no logical explanation for the chasm between reality and what appeared on film. Muggeridge insisted the building was divinely lit (the cameraman, meanwhile, put it down to a new type of film). From this experience and others, Muggeridge became a devotee of Mother Teresa. The following year, he published a book about her titled *Something Beautiful for God*. He is credited with being among the first to introduce Mother Teresa and her mission on the international stage.

After my volunteer shift, I wander over to the Kali temple next door, where dozens of goats are sacrificed each day to the goddess Kali as a *prasad* (blessed offering). Both the knife and the goat are bedecked in fresh flowers and draped in garlands of bright yellow marigolds. The animal must be decapitated in one clean motion, the guide says by rote, as it's believed to be the most humane. Its blood will be drained and poured into a decorative bowl, the centerpiece of a platter teeming with fresh fruit and flowers.

The meat is then prepared and variously taken home by the family who brought the animal, sold cheaply afterward, or else donated to the temple kitchens that feed up to two thousand people each day. Many more goats are sacrificed on Tuesdays and Saturdays, said to be auspicious days for Kali.

THE MOTHER TERESA EFFECT

She inspired us to sponsor a local school. And with the help of others, the children are fed a nutritious breakfast and a hot lunch.

THE GUTIERREZ FAMILY, GUATEMALA CITY

Our neighbor works the night shift and has to sleep during the day. The other moms and I have a roster to take her kids after school so that she can sleep a bit longer. It's only once a week each, but it makes a difference.

BRITTANY, QUEBEC

Saturday, December 7, 1996

I join others on laundry duty. Sheets, blankets, and clothes are scraped of incontinence, then swirled by hand or stick in two large concrete tanks. Stains are scrubbed by hand. Some men climb on the rim of the tank, squatting and thrashing about the soapy contents. Joe, an accountant from Estonia, tells me his thighs ached the first few days. He muses that at home right now, he'd be forging a path through knee-high snow, but here he's drenched in sweat, from both the work and the weather. Occasionally, others jump in and stamp on the sheets. They remind me of old movie scenes of grape stomping.

We wring out the blankets in pairs. It's a workout, and yet there is joy in it. Everything is hung on lines on the rooftop or spread out along the corrugated roof sheeting. This is fine in summer, but it takes days for the laundry to dry in winter and even longer through monsoon season. Someone with a German accent suggests to a nun that they buy industrial dryers and washers, but she cheerfully dismisses it, and gently reminds us all of the sisters' vow of poverty. Doing things by hand, she says, makes it easier for nuns and volunteers alike to better relate to the poor.

We sort donated medical gloves that are to be reused; so much for being disposable. This is concerning given the variety of illnesses, including tuberculosis, and the chance of cross-contamination. I wonder how nurses and doctors feel when they work here, accustomed to such strict standards of hygiene. Needles are reused after being run under cold water. They are then stored in a "sharps" container for safe disposal.

❧

As I write this at my desk back at the convent, a "house girl" (actually a young adult) is sweeping the floor. She disappears and then returns with water for bathing. I try to motion to her *thank you, but I can do it myself*. It's one thing to carry water for the elderly ladies, but it doesn't feel right that she's doing it for me. I follow her down the corridor for the second bucket, but she smiles and waves me off. Auntie Grace has arranged this, horrified that I'd been hauling my own water. Does she think I have domestic staff at home?

THE MOTHER TERESA EFFECT

As a child, I begged my parents to change my date of birth from August 27 to August 26 so that I could share my birthday with Mother Teresa.   RASHMI, HOUSTON

We were watching a film on her, and it gave me an idea about my mother-in-law. My father-in-law had died eight months ago, and she was at a loss. She volunteered for meals-on-wheels, but was seeking something more. They showed a scene where Mother Teresa was holding a baby, and I suggested that she volunteer at the local NICU (neonatal intensive care unit). Now she goes twice a week, to hold these tiny bundles and pour her love into them.   HENG, SAN FRANCISCO

Monday, December 9, 1996

At Kalighat, I meet a volunteer from Tokyo called Momoka. She went to Nabo Jibon House yesterday. It's principally a home for mentally disabled orphans. On the weekends (usually Sundays), volunteers gather there to bathe and feed the street children.

It was amusing, she says, to see the children take such delight in getting soapy. (I smile, but the former child-protection worker in me shudders. I slip in a prayer that the children aren't at risk of inappropriate touching. Exceedingly rare, perhaps, but possible.) Finally, hair was shining, fingernails were trimmed, and little toes gleamed. It dismayed her, then, to have to dress the children in the same grimy dresses, T-shirts, and shorts they wore on arrival. "There was nothing else to wear," she says. We look at each other and wince in unison—how often have we stood in front of our bulging wardrobes at home and proclaimed, "I have nothing to wear"? My cheeks burn in shame. I picture a river of volunteers having identical experiences on Sundays and identical conversations on Mondays.

Momoka goes on to say that the children then lined up eagerly and were fed dahl, rice, and curry before dispersing into the streets. (*Dahl*, or *dal*, is a lightly spiced lentil dish, often referred to as "the poor man's protein.") The line, she notes, extended around the block. My mind wanders to the lines every December at department-store sales with their "doorbuster" prices on the latest gadgets and games.

∽⊱⊰∾

The power of touch. We're encouraged to directly engage with patients, touching them and showering as much affection as they're comfortable with.

Touch transcends language, religion, and socioeconomics. It melts away barriers, however briefly. I think back to the late 1980s, when Princess Diana made headlines worldwide for hugging an AIDS patient. In that moment, two worlds collided and borders dissolved into a common humanity. "I see you," her hug conveyed; "I see you in me." I see and feel the need here at Kalighat for the power of touch. Our patients are used to being dismissed and disparaged, more accustomed to people stepping away from them than engaging them.

I pause for a moment to take in the sight of a college girl bent over a woman in her seventies. The woman's eyes are milky with age and fatigue; her body, withered. The girl strokes her hair and touches her arm. She murmurs something in English; neither speak the other's language and still there is communication. Despite the half century between caregiver and patient, the dynamic is one of a loving mother fussing over her sick child. This scene, playing out in a tiny corner of India, is echoed around the world.

THE MOTHER TERESA EFFECT

My nan was big on Mother Teresa. I watched her online and she encouraged me to stop attaching morality to poverty. As in, Why should I help you? Are you lazy? You're young and fit; get a job.

CORA, DUBLIN

A coworker's son had just been diagnosed with autism. When she told me in the break room, I wanted to help her plug into all these sites and services. Then I realized she didn't need that, right then. She needed someone to listen. GRACIE, HALIFAX

Tuesday, December 10, 1996

A small group of volunteers arrives, all twenty-somethings straight from Italy. One bursts into tears and another quietly sobs as they look around. A long-term worker soothes them as they take in the skeletal figures and the ravaged bodies of the patients. The sisters often say that most people cry at least twice here: when they arrive and when they leave. The first are usually tears of shock, as we see today, and later, tears of gratitude for having been here at all.

I turn back to a patient. Multiple cloths, each a little thicker than a dish towel, are used as underwear, either tied on like diapers or fixed with a rudimentary belt. They're communal, as are the clothes. These very same cloths are used to wash beds, scrub floors, and dust windows.

I talk with another volunteer about it, and we find a sister. We offer to cover the cost of the underwear. She's appreciative, but says all donations go to a central fund and can't be targeted for anything in particular. We gently persist—what if we buy the underwear ourselves in a variety of sizes? She declines, saying the system works as it is. Mother Teresa keeps things uncomplicated. It brings to mind the saying *Live simply, so that others may simply live.*

The afternoon brings time for light massage. Some patients need turning to prevent bedsores, though they're so underweight I can't imagine any pressure building up. Others have hands and feet gnarled by arthritis. Volunteers use oil to rub weathered fingers, trying gently to coax them into yielding and extending a bit more. I spot one woman among the fifty doing exercises. The Home offers regular meals and a safe environment, but the lure to return to her family on the sidewalk also drives her.

THE MOTHER TERESA EFFECT

She inspired me to have a work wardrobe (wearing the same sari every day). Only kidding! Actually, she helped start a family tradition: when we eat out, we order an extra item take-out, and we give it to a homeless person. ISOBELLA, MADRID

We're a tiny business, and it was a big deal when we hired our first employee outside the family. My wife short-listed a disabled woman, and I've got to say, I had my doubts. Would you believe, that Sunday's church service was about looking past the person's exterior to the gifts they had inside. We hired her, and she's transformed how we run the office. L., SACRAMENTO

WEDDING CLASSIFIEDS

Thursday, December 12, 1996

My sister's birthday. Hopefully Jon remembers to send the card and present we packed before he left.

I stop by Rita's apartment, and I'm pleasantly surprised to find the family at a late breakfast; she usually logs exhausting hours at their business.

While chatting, my Hindu cousin, in his twenties, makes a casual remark that stops me in my tracks. He turns to his mother and says, "I think it's time you found me a wife." I laugh, certain he is joking. "I've been thinking the same thing," she replies. "Would you like to use a marriage broker, or shall we put an ad in the *Telegraph*?"

When a woman marries in India, she moves in with her husband's family. With this in mind, marriage ads are written to reflect the family's social standing, and in turn, the caliber of the bride they expect. That said, it's heartening to see the phrase "caste no bar" included in some ads. This means the family are open to a bride from a lower socioeconomic group. Rita fishes about for a back copy of the newspaper and finds the bride/groom classifieds, just two columns over from the car ads.

Bride wanted, 20–22. Must be fair [skinned] and convent educated. Groom will inherit a Mumbai apartment at 30. Groom's sister has a master's degree in French.

As I skim the paper, I see many ads that describe the brides-to-be as "homely," and I wonder how they feel about this. And there's always a qualifier: "homely, but kind"; "homely, but intelligent"; "homely, but knows song."

⚬⊱⟶

Some random observations of life in Calcutta:

The papers are full of letters to the editor and grievance columns, complaining about nondelivery of mail or items removed from parcels, especially checks.

The white pages of the phone book are in the men's names only; there are no initials for their wives to distinguish a couple or family. There are no yellow pages to be found. The lady who sold me the bundle of aerograms says the last directory was compiled about five years ago. There is talk that a company might bring back the yellow pages by the turn of the century.

Letters and postcards need to be franked, as stamps will be peeled off and sold.

The Missionaries of Charity are very resourceful; they print business cards on used metro tickets. The metro carries very fast announcements in Bengali and English, interspersed with Hindi rap music.
I want to write more, but I'm starting to fade.

THE MOTHER TERESA EFFECT

She shared. She would have shared her toys when she was little.

FLYNN AND SAMUEL

It was my fifth trip to India. My friend Liliana and I wanted to do something special for the kids, so we asked our tour leader to coordinate a visit to the Missionaries of Charity orphanage in Agra. It was the same day that we visited the Taj Mahal. I thought about the coincidence that the Taj Mahal and the Missionaries of Charity's centers are places for love and death.

We entered a room with probably twelve cribs full of babies sleeping. One missionary was there with us. A baby girl woke up and reached out her arms to be held. I couldn't resist. What a moment! I thought of Mother Teresa and her incredible love, which crossed castes, gender, and countries. I felt humbled and blessed. I left the center with a heart full of love and a new perspective on life. SOLEDAD, HOUSTON

Sunday, December 15, 1996

As we tackle the dishes after breakfast, it occurs to me that Mother Teresa has squatted on this same floor and rinsed dishes at this same sink.

Back at the convent, I hunt down some old newspapers, as all the talk this week about arranged marriages has piqued my curiosity.

BRIDE: 23, 171 cm [5'7"], only issue [only child], convent educated, fair skinned, polite . . .

GROOM: Well-reputed doctor, kind, widower, issueless [no children], 57, partial hearing handicapped. No caste or dowry. Owns two flats [apartments].

BRIDE: 22, medium complexioned, slim, B. Sc. (Hons.), good position, will resign if desired . . .

While some ads presumably embellish, a few stand out for their refreshing candor:

ALLIANCE sought for $ indep. woman, 27, 5'1", amp'd lower leg, barren, v. good companion.

THE MOTHER TERESA EFFECT

We volunteer at a soup kitchen once a month.   DUDE855, ANNAPOLIS

There's a reason that suicides peak around Christmas. People feel so lonely. We invite someone to join us on the day, or immediately before, and then make a concrete plan to see them in the New Year.

INNES, LISBON

Tuesday, December 17, 1996

The humidity seems worse than usual, so I forgo jeans and try on a lightweight cotton *salwar kameez*. It's a reasonably slim-fitting tunic to my knees, with light trousers underneath. The delicate peach and white embroidery is at odds with my clunky hiking boots, but, hey, there are no catwalks planned.

Today is hectic at Kalighat. At least once a month, there is a total spring-cleaning. Beds are moved, windows cleaned of inch-thick dust, and the air is filled with a haze of powdered bleach. I'm grateful that we have masks, but what about the patients?

A dozen of us clean the floor by hand, with no mops or brooms in sight.

⚬⊱⟞⊰⚬

Afterward, a house girl sees me coming through the convent gate and waves me over. I'm to see Auntie Grace immediately. I find her with a chest rash, having been bitten by some sort of insect. But that's not why she has summoned me.

She tells me she was visited by one of the religious brothers, who has a good friend in the police force. Apparently I have been noticed on the street outside the convent for my paler skin and (modest) Western clothing. Women being forced into prostitution is not uncommon, and rumors are surfacing again of a white-sex-slave ring; the paler the victim's skin, the more money her controllers demand. "At least she's too old to be sold into marriage," his friend reportedly said, trying to be helpful. (I am twenty-eight.) I take all this in, silent. I've read the headlines, watched news reports, and discussed it in my social-work course, but I've never heard my name included in the same sentence as a prostitution racket. I had traveled with the brothers my first few days, and they offer to accompany me again. I gratefully accept.

I'm slowly meeting more women at the convent, and a favorite is Pearl, a stroke survivor in her eighties. I get to feed her meals whenever I'm back in time. I spoon the curry and rice and try to coax her. As we go back and forth, I wonder what secrets she holds in her hunched, withered shell. I imagine her as a mischievous little girl, a young bride, and a busy mother with children playing at her feet.

Another, Audrey, has lost most of her eyesight due to diabetes, she says, which she interweaves with stories of her childhood about life under the British before independence in 1947. She, like almost all the women here, are very color conscious. The paler the complexion, the more powerful the social standing, she notes, with a hint of sadness. I apply extra foot lotion and say nothing, feeling she's on the brink of a disclosure.

Audrey was the darkest of her siblings and while loved, she also felt her parents' slight embarrassment at times. She pauses, stares into the mid-distance, and then shifts to a lighter tone. She recalls her and her sisters being sent to boarding school in the hills. At the beginning of each term, a trunk, or "tuck box" of sweets and treats would be loaded aboard the train with their regular luggage. It was intended to last until they returned home, but, she adds with a wink, it never did.

Outside, the convent grounds are filled with the play and laughter of some young visitors aged ten to sixteen. They're gorgeous, loving, and unpretentious. It's endearing, as they seem compelled to touch you in some way as they talk. Little fingers rest lightly on your forearm, pat your hands, or play with your hair. They ask me to bring some music tapes after dinner. They say I look like Steffi Graf, and while they're sincere, I have to laugh, as there couldn't be less of a resemblance. We both sport ponytails; it ends there. Tonight we watch a Hindu music show in the communal living room, featuring a huge man in a kaftan and turban, rap dancing.

I join Sister Sunita to shell peas for dinner. She has been here six months, so in a sense, we're both adjusting. Afterward, we walk through the grounds, which boast lovely gardens and a pond. She suggests I learn to fish (even their pastimes are biblical). The edges of the pond are clogged with all manner of trash, from discarded cooking utensils and food wrappers to plastic bags and bottles.

At dinner, I learn that the sisters no longer recognize their individual birthdays. Instead, they celebrate the feast days of the patron saints who inspired their religious names.

Happy feast day to you
God's blessings on you
We wish you much more
One hundred and four!

I must remember Grace's feast day on January 28. Her religious name was inspired by Saint Thomas Aquinas. Group gifts are favored over something for the individual, and chocolates seem a safe bet.

I get ready for bed. As I brush my teeth, I am grateful for the clean, running tap water we have at home. I miss cupping my hands to rinse my mouth.

THE MOTHER TERESA EFFECT

We take school supplies on vacation. All it takes is a little planning and 5 to 10 percent of our vacation budget. The kids help decide. The other day my daughter said, "Mama, I'll do this with my children one day."

ELIANNE, CARACAS

A couple moved next door, and their baby would not stop wailing. All day, all night. I was getting peeved. Then something made me remember the tattered suitcases when they moved in. I got a gift card to a pharmacy, and slipped it under their door anonymously with a note of welcome. That night, the wailing stopped.

CHARLOTTE (LOTTE), DENVER

Wednesday, December 18, 1996

I bump into an American volunteer, Julia, on the street. A simple "How are you?" is enough to open the floodgates, and she bursts into tears. The nuns at Shishu Bhavan have declined to accept an application from her and her husband to adopt a baby. It's not that they processed her paperwork and found it lacking; they declined to review it at all. At forty-one, she wondered if she is considered too old.

After being refused a second time, Julia lined up at Motherhouse to see Mother Teresa and appeal her case. She was shocked at the explanation she received, as it had less to do with her age and more to do with her nationality. "I'm sorry, child. Mother believes abortion is available too freely in your country," she had said (Mother Teresa often spoke of herself in the third person). Julia is distraught.

Mrs. Webber, the old lady whose room is opposite mine, is calling out to her husband in her sleep. He has been dead fifteen years. From 9:00 P.M. to 5:30 A.M., her wails echo off the walls.

THE MOTHER TERESA EFFECT

She took care of their physical needs but recognized their dignity as equally important. ESIN, ANKARA

My brother is an alcoholic under the guise of a party guy. I was reading one of her books when I thought, what hole inside him is he filling with liquor? We hadn't spoken in over a year, and it took a lot to knock on that door, but it's eased things. I can't make him go to meetings, but I can help him feel less lonely. JULIAN, MELBOURNE

Thursday, December 19, 1996

I flee morning Mass to run to the bathroom, and spend the morning in a tandem cycle of vomiting and dry retching. I don't know what I've picked up, but at least it's shown up on my day off. Almost every day at Kalighat, one of the volunteers is away with a virus of some sort, so I'm glad not to lose a day.

Thursdays are my day to catch up on writing.

When a patient dies at Kalighat, prayers are recited, and he or she is wrapped carefully and lovingly in a white sheet. A tag encircles the big toes, and the body is then placed in a small tiled room to await transport to the crematorium. A modest sign carries a powerful reminder: *I am on my way to Heaven.* I ask a sister permission to take a photo of a shrouded body in that room. To me, the scene sums up beautifully the final phase of a "good death." She hesitates a moment, then nods.

✂

I'm better by late afternoon and take a short stroll to get some air.

I see the convent ambulance in the driveway. Not only is it tiny and almost bare of medical equipment, it's full of fruit and vegetables from the market. Too bad if someone actually needs it in a medical emergency.

On the walk back to the convent, I take out my camera in the hopes of capturing a general street shot. Within seconds, I am surrounded by children, waving and wanting their photo taken.

Lying in bed, I try to imagine what it is like having no family photos. None. No toothless baby pictures. No photographic evidence of your youth, or the day you got married, or the day your child was born. As I drift to sleep, I imagine buying the world's stock of Polaroid film and traveling across India to give out loaded cameras. I'd call it *The Polaroid Project*.

THE MOTHER TERESA EFFECT

Mom made me say sorry when I broke my sister's doll. First I just said it to not get in trouble, but later I meant it.

GENNA, AGE 7, SANTA FE

My sister asked for donations to daughtersrising.org in lieu of gifts for her twenty-first birthday. She's passionate about fighting sex trafficking and empowering young girls to avoid the common traps. She's an inspiration. SANJAY, MUMBAI

Friday, December 20, 1996

Caroline the Kiwi, a lovely volunteer from New Zealand, has her final day today, and we put up Christmas decorations together. She has a great sense of humor and completely understands the Australia–New Zealand rivalry. (Sample: When you meet a Kiwi, ask them to count to ten, first, *to prove they can*; second, because they will count it as "four, five, *sux*"—or "four, five, *sex*." God bless, they can't seem to pronounce short *i* sounds.)

She gives me a map of Calcutta, marked with good restaurants and places to make collect calls, such as the Central Telegraph Office.

I smile to see that some of the long-term volunteers have picked up the Indian mannerisms, with the head tilting and the wrist flowing in the course of conversation. When we were naughty as children, we gauged Mom and Dad's anger by how fast their heads and wrists were moving. If all were flying, we knew we were in big trouble. It was worse than them calling out your full name.

∝⃝

In the evening I take dictation from Mrs. Mascarenhas, who wants to send a letter to her daughter in Europe. She's lucid, but goes off on myriad tangents, from cooking advice to life lessons to what she thinks will happen on her "stories" (her favorite soap operas on the radio). I wonder what her daughter will make of it, but I figure she will welcome the news no matter what it says. When the letter is complete, she signs it in her small, spidery handwriting. Her touch is so light, the ink barely registers on the paper. In contrast, you can turn over a page of my writing and it almost feels like braille.

THE MOTHER TERESA EFFECT

She inspired us to join Amnesty International (amnesty.org). If she can be a voice for lepers, we surely can send a few letters as a voice for political prisoners.   ALESKA AND JAROSLAW, KRAKÓW

She made me think about how lonely some people are. I take the bus to work, and the driver is a little too chatty. I don't mind a smile, but I don't need a conversation before 7:00 A.M. One day, I overhead him saying life was hard since his wife died. After that, I made the effort to exchange a bit more.   TONYA, ADELAIDE

———#———

PART III

(Mother Teresa's Last)
Christmas and New Year

MEETING MOTHER TERESA

Sunday, December 22, 1996

As Christmas approaches, a heightened spirituality is cast over Kalighat. Perhaps we're all reflecting more on why we're here. The atmosphere is made more somber as we realize this could be Mother's final Christmas. Though she soldiers on, she has been unwell and there is talk of heart problems. She had two heart attacks in the 1980s: the first in 1983 while visiting Pope John Paul II in Rome, and, six years later, a second one requiring a pacemaker. ("Or was it a 'peacemaker'?" asks a sister with a laugh. Convent humor.)

Motherhouse is buzzing when we arrive. I am here with a group of sisters from the convent, and we initially meld into the small crowd that seems permanently installed to greet its famous resident.

A wooden box near the front of the building proclaims "Mother Teresa MC: IN." It has a little sliding window to show the IN or OUT. It's just like the *Peanuts* cartoon, where Lucy's sign proclaims the doctor is IN. Another sign, tacked to the wall immediately outside her office, reads "Mother Teresa, MC. 8:00–12:00 and 3:00–6:00." I smile to think its plain, simple lettering is more suited to a drab government building than to the office of one of the most famous women in the world.

I am afforded a few minutes alone with Mother Teresa. I take a sharp breath as it dawns on me that this is the woman who inspired my trip in the first place. My first impression is that she's even smaller than she appears on television. I feel as though I could slip her in my front pocket.

She offers me a rosary fashioned out of colored string and blesses it. Her novices make these rosaries by the batch, and they are given to everyone.

I pass along my aunt's regards, and we chat a little before she notices my wedding ring. "Oh, you're married?" she says. Such a simple question, and yet so loaded. "Yes, Mother, three years," I reply, almost automatically—and my heart sinks; I know what is coming next.

"And no children?" she intones.

I stare at her, mute. (Jon and I don't have kids. We forgot.) She has seen and heard it all and pauses only a moment before getting to the point.

"You take that pill, don't you?" she asks, eyebrow arched, though already knowing the answer as she studies my face.

I stare at my shoes. Dumbfounded, I still can't find my tongue. Was I really discussing family planning with Mother Teresa? No one hopes to impress her; you simply hope to not mess up. And here I was, messing up on a grand scale.

She comes a little closer, determined to leave no wiggle room. "Child, you take that pill to stop getting pregnant."

I see my chance.

"Well, Mother, I don't always take it. Sometimes I balance it between my knees."

Her face freezes in shock, and thoughts spin in my head. *She's had a stroke. You've killed her. You've actually killed Mother Teresa.* And then: *This will not look good on a résumé.* I begin to lurch forward to call for help, but I am rooted to the spot.

In that moment, she throws her head back, and she laughs. Obviously, it doesn't signal approval; it is simply a release from having been startled.

I'm not hanging around. I kiss her hands, thank her, and leave. [She died nine months later, but let me clarify: it wasn't me.]

Earlier in the day we'd made a few other stops, but I'll write about them later. I want to let the experience of meeting her wash over me. I lie on my bed and replay the conversation in my head. I don't recall doing this since I had a crush on a boy in high school.

THE MOTHER TERESA EFFECT

We are seniors at a boarding school. We collected money to send to an orphanage in Bolivia. Those kids are the ages of our younger brothers and sisters.   ELAINE, PRIYANKA, AND DEANNA, BOSTON

Each week, we prepay for one of those bags of groceries at the supermarket designated for the needy.   B. AND T., OMAHA

Monday, December 23, 1996

I didn't sleep much last night, playing and replaying the experience of having met Mother Teresa. Despite feeling a bit foggy, I'm up early and head back to Motherhouse. I'll go to Mass there today instead of at the convent as usual.

I take a seat in a little vacant spot on the floor. I am astonished when Mother arrives a moment later and sits directly in front of me, also sitting cross-legged. Yesterday I had startled her; now she returns the favor. I exchange glances with the volunteer next to me: *Can you believe this?* Mother is petite, and her sari billows around her like a sheet. From behind, she looks like a crumpled pile of laundry. She is barefoot, but I look for her sandals the way one would expect to see Gandhi in his glasses. It occurs to me only later that we had all removed our shoes before entering the chapel.

After Mass, volunteers are provided tea (no eggplant infusion!), bananas, and a medley of white bread and *chapattis* (flat bread).

⤝⤞

Catching up on yesterday: Mother Teresa was the headline, but we had a busy day before that.

We began the morning in Howra, about twenty minutes away, where the sisters have another convent. It's a stone's throw to the slums of Pilkhana, said to have inspired the book *City of Joy* by Dominique

Lapierre (1985) and the movie of the same name in 1992. I take in a conversation with interest. One man recalls there were protests during filming, as locals anticipated how the film might portray the poor. Another wishes the sets had been left intact rather than tearing them down; they would have provided sturdy accommodation for pavement dwellers. A sister remarks that the filmmakers were very generous with their donations to the poor.

The neighborhood is "very India"—a cross-section of goats wandering the alleyways and in front of stores, men spitting, and street children everywhere. Vendors hawk their wares and everywhere—*everywhere*— people live cheek by jowl along open sewers, stores, and homes.

We then stopped at Shishu Bhavan, a home for children up to age ten, but I see mainly babies and toddlers. I'm looking forward to return- ing for a shift or two. My volunteer ID card shows Kalighat, but they let me through as I'm with the nuns. Dozens of babies stare through the bars of individual cots. Many were relinquished by their families due to physical or mental disabilities. Others are healthy baby girls who are sadly viewed as liabilities, as they'll need a dowry one day. They are bare bottomed, and we simply clean up after them in the absence of diapers. Sometimes supplies have run low, or they're left diaperless to give a rash some fresh air.

The babies arrive here in various ways. Often, the parents simply can- not look after them due to crushing poverty. Other times, the mother dies in childbirth or the stigma of an infant born out of wedlock proves too much. Occasionally, a two- or three-year-old is found tied to a small pole in the gate until the sisters open for the day. At least once that I learned of, a toddler abandoned at the gate was mauled by a dog; a vol- unteer was so incensed, she took a photo of the child's bloodied face and had it blown up into posters around the neighborhood, trying to shame the parents. "I don't judge them for giving her up," she said, "but I can't forgive them for just leaving her there."

Trying to amuse them, I sing (badly) an old folk song about kooka- burras (Australian kingfisher birds). Of course, they have no idea what I'm saying, but most smile and gurgle. One stares blankly, unimpressed. Everyone's a critic.

There are toys for the children to play with, but they tend to be poor quality and meager. I know the sisters are doing their very best, but it's hard to take in. I think of the boys back at our boarding school in Perth. I wish they could experience this to better appreciate all they have. Among our sixty teenagers are several brothers, who happen to be princes. I remember when they showed us photos of their recreation room in the palace, complete with scaled-down sports cars. Their youngest brother, aged ten, was found with five thousand dollars' cash in his pocket. "Dad thought I might need some extra money" was his astonishing reply. At our sister school for girls, his sister and cousin presented their favorite teacher with a top-of-the-line BMW, until the principal intervened.

THE MOTHER TERESA EFFECT

We run an interfaith prayer group, and we're inspired that she welcomed and cared for others with no regard to their religion, or lack of one. POALA, FLORENCE

I think it is important to help the poor because they don't have as much as we do. LIVINIA, AGE 8, PERTH

CHRISTMAS

Tuesday, December 24, 1996

Kalighat is packed today with sixty volunteers, most here today and gone tomorrow. It's actually too congested, and as happy as you are to orient them, you sigh because they'll depart so soon. It's chaotic and lacks any system. But Christmas carols are being sung everywhere, and the atmosphere is heartening.

Christmas morning will begin at Kalighat around 6:30 A.M., when I meet Tess and others to sort treats before the regular day gets underway. There's still breakfast to do, and then Mass will be at 10:00 A.M. That will be followed by lunch for the patients, then a meal for the volunteers. Some of us will stay on to do the cooking for dinner, because most of the staff will be off duty. There will be no sisters here on Boxing Day (December 26) as that's the day *they* celebrate Christmas.

I think of the journalist Malcom Muggeridge and his belief that Kalighat was divinely lit. If each living person or thing has a vibration, then it makes sense to me that decades of love and compassion inside these walls would render a spiritual impression. And as we're reminded, the building was originally a dormitory for Hindu pilgrims to the temple next door. I look around and imagine a mingling of prayer and good intention swirling above us.

As we prepare to wrap up our day and head outside, a sister urges us "to see the Holy Family among those on the sidewalk . . . just as Mary and Joseph found no room at the inn, so too these people feel turned away."

<hr />

I'm back at the convent and getting ready for "Midnight Mass"—at 9:00 P.M. Well, I guess it's midnight somewhere. The nuns resonate serenity. Tonight, though, Auntie Grace got very stressed. I wore a white camisole with a long-sleeved shirt over it and as the white peeked through, she worried that I was "showing [my] undergarments to all and sundry." Oh, Auntie.

Despite the festive air, the female residents at the convent are squabbling among themselves. Much of it, I imagine, is rooted in a lack of privacy. Everyone lives in such close proximity to everyone else that it's only natural that it would take its toll.

Across town, some volunteers are leading a candlelight procession to Motherhouse, singing carols. No one knows if Mother Teresa will attend, as she is unwell. When the crowd gathers in the courtyard of Motherhouse, a nativity play is presented. To everyone's delight, Mother appears at the balcony and waves to those below.

THE MOTHER TERESA EFFECT

Twice a year, we have a cleanout and donate the clothes to Goodwill
(goodwill.org).   THOMAS, NEW YORK CITY

Our local senior center has nice food, but it's so repetitive. Once a
month, our group takes afternoon snacks inspired by a different coun-
try. We give a short talk, and sometimes members of a local youth group
will learn a dance from that country to go with it.   JOYCE, BRISBANE

Wednesday, December 25, 1996

A few of us have organized a giant sheet cake for the patients and sisters.
Tess and I try to get a taxi to the bakery, and the man insists on charging
us four times the going rate, so we give up for the time being. It's not
that you begrudge them the extra money, but this endless replay of petty
rip-offs leaves you drained. Others are organizing sweets, fresh fruit, and
myriad treats. We pool everything and dole some candy into blue bags
for patients to enjoy at their own pace later.

The MC Brothers sit on blue sheets on the floor, singing Christmas
hymns and beating drums. Red and gold tinsel is draped around the windows. One volunteer is dressed as Santa, another as an angel. A nativity
scene is set up in the front area, with a small Christmas tree to the side.

After lunch, we begin to hand out a modest assortment to each
patient. I offer a slice of cake, some soft candy, and a small tangelo to a
woman, and her response takes me aback. "All for me?" she asks in Hindi.
"Are you sure this is all for me?" I swallow hard and look away to the
novice who is translating.

One couple got engaged here, apparently after dating just one month.
He dressed as an angel last night for Christmas Eve and was photographed
for the paper, posing over a street child.

In the laundry, I'm paired with Patrick, an athletic, multilingual opera
singer who is training to be a Jesuit priest. Some people are so talented,

it's sickening; I like him instantly. He gets to work, squatting on the edge of the concrete tanks.

∝—◯

Rita tells me of some people in Calcutta—Anglo-Indians, like us—who are more British than the British. They host full traditional English Christmas dinners in the stifling Indian humidity, complete with plum pudding and brandy custard. But because they don't see how Indians in Britain adapt, they're almost preserved in time: a sort of social formaldehyde.

THE MOTHER TERESA EFFECT

Every day when I come home, I dump my keys and my change in a bowl by the door. I bag up the coins and give them to street people.
MARC, CAPE TOWN

Everyone knows what it's like to be on the outside. New job, new school, new club. A warm welcome takes moments, but makes such a difference.
DOROTHEA, SYDNEY

Thursday, December 26, 1996

I wait for a call from Jon at 7:00 A.M.—no luck; he couldn't get through. I head to Kalighat.

A new patient has terribly misshapen feet and to add to it, her toes are infected. Someone brushes past her bed and leaves her in agony. The cots are the patient's one claim to privacy and personal space. Each will sleep on it, eat on it, socialize from it. It is a bed, a dining area, an examination table, and a sort of front parlor to receive visitors. I imagine it becomes their world.

∝—◯

At the convent, I'm advised to eat the yellow pith of a pomegranate to stave off another stomach bug.

The residents are always popping into my room for chats, especially the two ladies on either side of me. It's like having ninety mothers. *Have you eaten properly? Did you skip breakfast? Why are you looking so tired? I think I have some vitamins . . .* (as they rummage around their handbags, which invariably produce nothing but crumpled tissues and the occasional mint). I know they mean well, but it's becoming a little stifling.

THE MOTHER TERESA EFFECT

I mentor. She saw gifts in others, and I try to do that too, nurturing the next wave of female engineers.   CELIA, BUDAPEST

I saw the moving vans roll up and took pizzas to our new neighbors, and the delivery guys. It cost very little but got us off to a good start.
                                                          SERGEI, FORT LAUDERDALE

Saturday, December 28, 1996

I enlist two of the women residents to help pick up chocolates and pastries for the convent. The bakery staff has bungled the order again, as they did a few weeks ago. The quality is good and the men are pleasant enough, so as frustrated as I feel, I try to overlook their lack of organization.

Speaking of sweets, ice cream vans sell regular-size cones, but with only a teaspoon of actual ice cream. I think they'd pass out if I requested a whole scoop. I look down at this comically paltry serving and wonder what they would say at home.

Auntie Grace has suffered a fall, but is better now, her bruised chin beginning to heal.

Though she is long retired as a Mother Superior, Auntie Grace still considers the nuns her charges. She reminds the Sister Superior to wear a hair clip to keep the hair out of her eyes—the woman is in her fifties!

Another nun has a tuft of curls poking out of her veil at morning Mass, and Auntie gives herself a migraine, worrying that it's improper. But they're all fond of her and humor her with loving patience.

My cousins head to a party. One pays the band to walk home with him while he dances down the street. He will leave soon to attend college in Australia; he's in for a shock, as he won't be able to buy favors half as easily there, nor have domestic staff at his beck and call.

THE MOTHER TERESA EFFECT

She motivated us to do the World Vision's 30-Hour Famine (30hour famine.org). It's once a year, but now we do it on our own once a quarter—the first day of winter, the first day of spring, etc. It does a soul good to remember what hunger feels like, and it's a mini spiritual retreat as time marches on and the leaves fall or the weather warms.

LENA AND T., BOSTON

I'm an internist. Last year I dropped to four days a week to volunteer Friday mornings at a free clinic.   LIZ, PALO ALTO

Sunday, December 29, 1996

The sisters are hosting a delegation from out of town right now, for a series of meetings scheduled through the holiday period.

Indian hospitality being what it is, the lunch table groans with all manner of curries, pickles, and chutneys. The visitors, fresh from their own Motherhouse in Europe, each take a bite, and I watch with interest. As if on cue, each woman turns bright red, and little beads of sweat appear at her hairline. "Is something wrong?" the Sister Superior asks with a furrowed brow. The most senior nun dabs the corner of her mouth with a napkin, taking a moment to gather her thoughts. "It's delicious. It's simply that we cook with two spices at home: salt and pepper." Boiled potatoes quickly appear—and I secretly rejoice.

The visitors invite me to join them on a day trip next week to the island of Basanti ("bah-SHAN-thee"). I make a mental note to ask the sister at Kalighat to swap my day off.

The last few nights have been Muslim festivals. All day and night, huge firecrackers go off—except that they sound like miniature bombs. The noise continues without a break until dawn.

THE MOTHER TERESA EFFECT

Ask "How are you?" and actually listen to the answer.   AIKO, KYOTO

Every winter, I buy eight to ten sleeping bags and give them out to the people who live under the bridges.   OLIVER, LONDON

Monday, December 30, 1996

Jackpot! There are eight pieces of mail waiting for me when I get home from Kalighat, including a handmade Christmas card.

I set off on a wild goose chase to find Auntie some more of her knee-high stockings.

When I get back, the second floor is buzzing with the sounds of women gossiping. It seems Mrs. Webber's house girl has been physically and verbally abusing her. It's news to some—including me—while others have known for a while. Why on earth would they stay silent? The lady herself won't discuss it. I go to the Sister Superior, who in turn talks to Mrs. Webber, but she refuses to make any accusations. I want to blast the house girl, but I don't speak Bengali.

An Anglo-Indian family visits to sing hymns for the residents and takes requests for popular songs. And by that, I mean songs popular in the 1940s and '50s.

THE MOTHER TERESA EFFECT

We were moving overseas and instead of selling our car, we donated it to a family in need. I can still see the mother's face.

ANNUNZIATA, ROME

Don't ask someone, "Do you want this?" It makes them feel like a charity case. Ask, "Would you like this?" or "Do you know someone who could use this?"

ISAAC, TEL AVIV

Tuesday, December 31, 1996

At Kalighat, breakfast is being prepared as usual when a volunteer has a meltdown. She throws down a plate and bursts into tears. "What's the point?" she laments. "Nothing changes. One dies, and another takes the bed, even more skeletal." Christina is a nursing student from England, and has been here about two months. She is angry the Home isn't more like a hospital. These past few days she has been tending a woman who was coughing up blood, and felt helpless as she watched her suffer.

A nun sits with her, listens, and lets her vent without interrupting. She has seen it before. I hear the sister say, "We can't do great things. We can only do small things with great love." She is quoting Mother Teresa. The two head upstairs for some fresh air; Christina decides to take the day off and will try again tomorrow.

⌒⌒

Afterward, I take a tram and then an auto-ric to see my Auntie Dulcie, who is visiting from Perth. It's lovely to spend time with her and to hear news from home. As I hug her, I enjoy a waft of her signature perfume, and I'm transported back to childhood. Aromas mingle; the house smells of sandalwood soap and incense.

I've not felt any real homesickness, but the first pang surfaces when I hear Jon's voice tonight.

Father Morton, a visiting priest, shows a film in the common room this evening. It's about religious life, and I slip out after a respectable time. It's not that the movie is dull, but I see religious life play out every day here, and I prefer it unfolding right in front of me.

My cousin calls to invite me to not one but *four* parties—the first in their building and then three hosted by different friends. I'm tempted, but I've been "volunteered" to attend Special Prayers and choir practice. I don't mind, but they'll regret recruiting me when they hear me sing. I think of friends at home, heading out to crammed bars with live music blaring until dawn.

THE MOTHER TERESA EFFECT

Boast about someone else and their achievements.   DIWATA, MANILA

I'm planning a gap year before grad school. I've signed up to volunteer at a couple of orphanages in Central America.   JANA, BOISE

Wednesday, January 1, 1997

Christina is back.

No one says anything about yesterday. They just hug her, which says plenty.

THE MOTHER TERESA EFFECT

Don't hold grudges. She spoke about forgiveness, and it got me thinking of the price we pay when we hold onto hurt.   ROLF, COPENHAGEN

We foster older children, who are more difficult to place.

EVA, SANTIAGO DE CHILE

Thursday, January 2, 1997

This evening I stop by Rita's apartment to pick up some errant mail, and I catch her on the way to a dinner. I gasp as I take in her outfit. She is always beautifully groomed but not ostentatious. Tonight, she is dripping in diamonds and gold. She explains that many of the other guests will have daughters of marriageable age, and through her dress, she will signal she can support the daughter of a good family. This gives her son the best chance to find a wife.

I've worked through the first forty aerograms and take a stroll to buy another fifty. This time, the woman at the postal counter trusts that I know what I want, and we skip the pantomime. On the way back, I absorb the cacophony of sound. The blaring horns eventually become white noise, but there are layers beneath that: the loudspeakers from temples, the stores blasting music, and the street vendors shouting in the time-honored tradition of a town crier. The car fumes can leave you dizzy at times.

I'm convinced that I'm constantly on the verge of stepping in something. Psychologists must have a term for this condition. At least while I'm looking down, there's less chance of stumbling on the crumbling sidewalks and breaking an ankle.

THE MOTHER TERESA EFFECT

There's this guy on my way to work who's always got a cup out. I asked his name, and now we eat lunch once a month, on payday. He sees me coming and clears a milk crate so I can take a seat.

LUCAS, NEW YORK CITY

Be kinder and more patient than people deserve. IRMA, SAN ANTONIO

Friday, January 3, 1997

I am invited to join the nuns on a day trip to Basanti. I happily tag along and welcome the chance to escape the city and embrace the countryside. It's a four-hour journey each way. We're grateful the driver insisted we bring cushions; we seem to hit every pothole on the road. But we're also treated to views of rice paddies and fields of hay and sugarcane, which is a delight. The van rumbles by two women maneuvering a huge amount of hay on their heads; they look like a walking bale with legs.

Basanti is actually an island. We cross the water on a rickety boat with standing room only, but the journey itself takes minutes.

There is a convent here, and also a girls' school. The hospitality is poignant; generosity of spirit is truly a mindset, not a tax bracket. The resident nuns bestow floral garlands around our necks, provide a delicious meal, and give us a tour of the grounds. Some of them are also nurses, and there is a visiting doctor.

We tour a school, chapel, and lake area. The gardens are simple but lush and striking in design. There is also a hospital with twenty-five beds.

We meet a teenage girl, horrifically burned after a boy threw acid in her face for declining his romantic interest. Her face is disfigured, the skin bleached and melted into patterns, yet she smiles and chats. In fact, she *glows*. It is humbling to see the triumph of the human spirit through her charred shell. I cannot imagine the pain she has endured, both physically and emotionally. How easy it might have been for her to become bitter or to lament her diminished chance at marriage, and yet here she is, laughing.

The surgical area is threadbare, and a large blood stain in the concrete floor gives me pause. The operating table is little more than a sheet of steel, and the bench beside it has green peeling paint. There is no kind of extra lighting for the surgeons. I wonder if they have a backup generator in the event of power loss during a procedure.

We stop at a market on the way out of town. Fish is laid out on newspaper in the sun, and there are dozens and dozens of chickens in cane cages. Men play cards in the dirt (trash talk sounds the same in every language), and children wander among it all. Three men in their thirties are very amused at the stockings the nuns wear, pointing and giggling like children.

We pass the saddest-looking circus on the way home. The tent is made of worn canvas, brightly colored but tattered. An old, tired elephant is pegged outside with no shade from the sun and little water. If there were ever a case for animals on antidepressants, this is it.

It's another four hours back to the city.

THE MOTHER TERESA EFFECT

We collect lightly used toys for foster kids. We also try to include a new one here and there, because it's so rare they get a brand new doll or game. MEL, PHOENIX

I'm an attorney, and for years I've been hosting a free legal clinic at a community center. This year, my daughter graduated and joined me. ARUSHI, CHENNAI

Saturday, January 4, 1997

I'm writing in the washroom, as it's the only place with light. We're encouraged not to use electricity between 8:00 A.M. and 8:00 P.M.

Kalighat is overflowing with volunteers again. A new group of ten and another of twenty-five arrive for the day—you help orient them, and then they're gone. I crave some sort of system.

The extra hands give me a chance to talk with one of the sisters. I relish the opportunity, as they tend to be very private. I wonder how old she was when she got her calling, but it seems too personal a topic. Instead, I keep it light and ask about the saris. She says each sister gets three: one to wear, a second to launder, and a third to repair if need be. "I'll be buried in one of them," she remarks candidly. They also receive a rosary, a crucifix, a bucket, and a brush among their personal items. Another volunteer stops by to invite her and the other sisters to dinner tonight; she declines and explains that they eat only what the convent provides. This embraces their vow of poverty and keeps their lifestyle more aligned to the poor. (For the same reason, Motherhouse has no air conditioning.)

⚬✂⚬

As I arrive back at the convent, a funeral service is in progress for a former resident. Here, death is looked in the eye, acknowledged as part of life. That said, the terminology is a little different. No one "dies"; they "expire." There is no fancy coffin nor embalming. The woman's body has been laid out in the front parlor these past few days, dressed as she would be in life and equally as visible to visitors as to the mailman. Seemingly the only concession to death is the cotton balls stuffed into her nostrils. Overall, the look is quite natural—except for her hands, which are positioned oddly on her chest, like kangaroo paws.

I pop by to see Auntie Grace, and she has some handwritten notes by her side; she has been expecting me. She has jotted down a few more memories of Mother Teresa. Mother needed to travel as she set up more homes in India and overseas, she tells me. The national rail company gave her a lifetime free pass, which helped enormously. But then over time, international travel became more pressing. She staggered her colleagues by writing to a major airline—and offering to work as an air hostess on the long-haul flights if she could travel at no charge! Imagine Mother Teresa coming by with the drinks trolley or asking, "Chicken or fish?" Grace says the nuns teased Teresa at length about this, but she remained steadfast.

Speaking of air travel, Mother Teresa took action on a 1980s TACA Airlines flight to Mexico City, which will be long remembered by all aboard. She was just about to be served lunch when she asked the flight attendant the cost of her meal. The woman checked, and informed her that it cost around one dollar. "If I don't eat it, will you give me the dollar for the poor?" she asked. The startled attendant checked with the pilot and assured her she could have the money. Mother's travel companion on that flight was Bob Macauley, founder of AmeriCares (americares.org). Of course, he offered to do the same and soon the whole flight had volunteered to give up their meals. This meant Mother Teresa had $129 to feed the poor—but she wasn't quite done. She asked Bob to round up the meals and convinced the airline to organize a truck! She and Bob then delivered the meals to a shanty town. He recalled the hair-raising journey, as Mother was so short, she could barely see above the wheel.

Not everyone was as enamored immediately with Mother Teresa. Grace also shares a story which I recall my father telling us as children. She had just established Shishu Bhavan, the children's home, and money was always tight. She visited a local baker and asked him to donate bread. In response, the man spat at her. Mother Teresa remained composed and said, "I will take that for me. But what can you offer the children?" He became a regular donor to the orphanage.

THE MOTHER TERESA EFFECT

I'm a hairdresser and I volunteer twice a month at a nursing home. It's less about the cut and more about the pampering. JOJO, MANCHESTER

Whenever Mother Teresa was on the news, Dad would call us inside. For years, he apprenticed young mechanics and took pride in helping those kids get started. His garage was in a rough part of town, and to many of them, he was a father figure. ALEX, SÃO PAULO

Monday, January 6, 1997

At Kalighat, I meet some Danish girls who are fresh from a backpacking trip across the US. As we chat during the break, one produces a piece of paper from her pocket with a sly smile. It's a news article on the "Nun Bun," a cinnamon roll that bears a striking resemblance to Mother Teresa. And it really does, with the layers of pastry forming the folds of her sari and the wrinkles of her face. It was discovered at a café bakery in Nashville, Tennessee. The girls say it's been featured on all the talk shows in the US. They show the sisters and share a laugh; Mother is aware of it and finds it amusing.*

⊶

I'm in my room when one of the house girls slips a note under my door from Auntie Grace. She has decided to undertake an eight-day silent retreat ("a little one, in my room"). She writes:

> *An annual retreat is a time to review the past year, whether we have cooperated with the graces God has given us, or not. Theologians say that in our spiritual life, we don't stand still. Day by day we either improve or we don't.*

In fact, most of the nuns are on retreat. Mealtimes are held in silence, with the sisters using hand gestures to signal what they need or think. I follow in clumsy imitation. The pointing is clear enough, but I swear that some look as though they're about to land a plane, and I have no idea what they mean.

THE MOTHER TERESA EFFECT

I collect smiles on the metro. Yes, I'm that guy. HENRI, PARIS

Mom noticed a pizza truck delivering almost every day to her new neighbors across the road. She'd see teenagers come and go, but never a proper adult. It turned out their parents had died in a car accident, and the nineteen-year-old was holding it together—even applying for guardianship of her younger siblings. Mom took them under her wing, helped them get organized with school and on a cooking schedule. It's been two years, and she still checks on them. BROOKE, CLEVELAND

---

* She later wrote to the Nashville café, asking that they not sell "Mother Teresa Miracle Nun Bun" merchandise. The owner graciously complied and shortened the name to "Nun Bun," which is now trademarked.

Tuesday, January 7, 1997

Scams thrive anywhere tourists gather, and Calcutta is no exception. A popular one here involves powdered milk. A woman sits outside a store with a baby in her lap (who could be hers, borrowed for the day, or part of an organized ring). She begs for coins for milk to feed her infant, or asks that you go inside to buy her a packet of powdered milk. When you're gone, she returns the packet, and collects her cut from the store-keeper. This continues, the same packet carried in and out between store and sidewalk, becoming more dog-eared as the day wears on. Children are sometimes physically maimed to attract more money. Legs or arms are broken and left to set, misshapen and gnarled, to attract more dona-tions. We see youngsters who have been blinded; the sisters say it is done with anything from bleach to brutish gouging.

In another ruse, children follow you, waving pens or slipping flower bracelets around your wrist. They speak three words of English: "It's a gift." Of course, you're fishing about for money before you know it.

THE MOTHER TERESA EFFECT

I wheel in my neighbor's trash can.   BRAD, PORTLAND

I was given one of her books, and it changed my perspective on how I was handling my kids. I was giving them too much after a bit-ter divorce, unconsciously buying their affection. I realized I was not doing any of us any favors, and I began to ease back. Yes, they whined initially, but today they appreciate the occasional treat much more.

BETHANY, TULSA

Wednesday, January 8, 1997

Rita takes me to the Saturday Club for coffee. The waiter is an older, distinguished gentleman who regales us with stories of how Princess Margaret once came and ordered a waterfall of gin and tonic.

An accomplishment of sorts today at the convent: Mrs. Webber, directly opposite me, has a house girl who treats her very badly. She tells me the girl beats her, harangues her, and starves her of food (as punishment for having to toilet her). And she threatens Mrs. Webber if she tells anyone. Another resident, Marie, and I have gone to the Sister Superior, to no avail. No one else wants to be involved, so they say they don't hear or see anything untoward. We went to see the sister again today, revealed everything, and, crucially, Marie convinced Mrs. Webber to speak up.

The Sister Superior gave the girl a severe dressing down and sacked her on the spot. Unfortunately, she then lied, saying that she had left something in Mrs. Webber's room—and twisted the poor woman's arm severely as a parting gesture. The staff think it's fractured in two places. The old lady has now been assigned a caring, gentle girl, and has been moved downstairs so she can be wheeled into the garden when the sun is out. This also means the sisters can more closely monitor her. I feel sick that the abuse went on so long.

❦

British Prime Minister John Major is in town, so traffic is even worse than normal. Of course, he's staying at one of Calcutta's finest hotels, and by coincidence a family friend works there. I remark to my cousin that she's a very attractive woman; he agrees and laments her not being able to marry right now. Her family has suffered a financial setback, he says, so it is hard to attract a husband from a good family.

As I read about Major's visit, I spot a headline about a postal strike. The mail system here is archaic. The workers threaten that for each day negotiations drag on, one ton of mail will be dumped into the sea. I imagine letters from home getting soggy and being read by an old fish wearing glasses, sitting on a rocking chair at the bottom of the ocean.

THE MOTHER TERESA EFFECT

Kids can stop you in your tracks. We told our teenager that whatever he could save for a car, we'd match up to a set amount. He had his heart set on a certain model. When he finally scraped enough together, I offered to start checking out used car lots. Out of the blue, he said he'd cut a quarter off the budget, and asked me to take the balance to an orphanage in South America next time I travel for business.

WILLIAM, BOSTON

Everyone goes on about cyberbullying, but I look for people who don't get many likes or comments, and I like their posts so that they know someone noticed.

MEI, KUALA LUMPUR

Thursday, January 9, 1997

Bollywood!

Rita spirits me away to a matinee film. The ticket line stretches out and we join the throng; it moves like molasses and gives me a chance to absorb the goings-on. A crush of people mill about, eating, gossiping, and stretching their legs before they'll sit cramped for several hours.

Inside, the theater seems to hold more than a thousand people, most noisy and chatty. Many are in seats, but others lean on balconies and crouch on steps; bodies are crammed into every crevice. The universal smell of popcorn mingles with samosas, sweat, and overpowering cologne.

I instinctively look for a way out in case a fire starts, but Rita is way ahead of me. "There," she says, pointing to an exit sign. She then hands me earplugs. "If you think the crowd is noisy now," she says . . .

As the curtains begin to part, half the audience makes a racket telling the other half to be quiet. Ads play and previews show, all with ear-splitting soundtracks in Hindi. Romance, death, and action movies seem to be the most popular, and the crowd screams their deafening approval whenever something explodes or bursts into flames. This is not passive entertainment, but a living, breathing barometer of approval, anger, or amusement.

Rita says moviegoers demand Bollywood films to be drawn out, with most at least three hours long. It's something affordable on a very modest wage and a major form of entertainment, she explains, for servants, office cleaners, and street vendors. And who could deny them that escapism? For those who can't read or write, movies offer even more. If patrons aren't pleased with the film's plot, music, or ending, they can unleash their fury on the theater; Rita has seen seats vandalized and curtains torn. On the other hand, if they love a film, moviegoers may think nothing of seeing it half a dozen times or more. It echoes the time-honored Indian tradition of storytelling, be it of myths or morals, which are told and retold through generations.

The movie gets underway with English subtitles. The colors are vivid, the music deafening, and seemingly every actor, from the leading couple to the peripheral characters, could moonlight as a model. I briefly spot a sage with facial warts; it seems his wisdom makes up for his homely features.

Core themes can be relied on, says Rita. The universal "boy-meets-girl" framework is a winner, as is the story of someone avenging a father or mother's death. City life is a favorite subject, along with romance and family dynamics. And there are multiple plots within plots. At seemingly random moments, songs are injected with stunning choreography and costumes laden with gold, sequins, and jewels. The crowd shouts and stamps their approval. Dream sequences are riotously popular, even as they abandon all logic and plot points. Adults and children sing along, some getting up in their seats until others shout them down.

In fact, the audience doesn't hesitate to interact with the characters on-screen. Villains are greeted with boos, while beautiful starlets make their entrance to catcalls and cheers. People shout out warnings to the damsel in distress, or cuss and abuse the evil, meddling mother-in-law. I've not seen much of this back-and-forth at home, except for perhaps *The Rocky Horror Picture Show* or the occasional *Sound of Music* sing-along.

For all the romance, build-up, and drama, the film is very chaste. The lead couple seem permanently on the verge of a passionate embrace—but never quite get there. Instead, she kisses a tree, and the crowd roars. He kisses the tree, and they swoon. (Yet outside, erotic art abounds on the streets, in museums, even in temples.)

It's an exhausting but vivid experience.

✄

Jon calls and he's feeling down. He says writing letters reinforces the distance between us, whereas I feel the opposite. I know he wants to ask me to come home, and I love him even more for not doing it. Instead, we decide to call twice a week: we'll aim for Wednesdays and Sundays.

THE MOTHER TERESA EFFECT

See past the homelessness to the person inside. That someone's baby boy or girl.   SAJIDA, LOS ANGELES

It was Father's Day, and Dad said what he really wanted was for us to go to church together as a family, like we did growing up, so we did.   LIAM, TAMPA

Friday, January 10, 1997

I receive a fax from Jon, a lovely surprise after talking last night.

A volunteer arrives at Kalighat from Shishu Bhavan (the home for babies and children). She says two women have been asked to leave after they were overheard discussing contraception.

A visiting religious brother at Kalighat is a wonderful juggler and entertains the patients. This reminds me of a favorite book as a child, about the lives of the saints. It told the tale of Saint Barnabus, who joins an abbey and struggles from day one. He can't sing in chapel, he can't work the farm, and he's hopeless as a gardener. He wrings his hands, not knowing how to serve. One day, the abbot catches him standing on his head while juggling in front of a statue of the Virgin Mary and the infant Jesus. He is about to rebuke Barnabus when the baby comes alive and claps in delight at the spectacle. The old man shrinks away; he allows Barnabus to offer whatever gifts he has.

THE MOTHER TERESA EFFECT

She didn't care about someone's skin color, or religion, or even if they were a good person. She just helped. IMRAN, KARACHI

I grew up reciting all the formal prayers in school and church, but she made me realize we can talk to God as we do a good friend.
CAROLINA-MARIA, TIJUANA

Monday, January 13, 1997

After a dry spell, three letters arrive from home, including one from the parents of a childhood friend.

Rita takes me to a fancy hotel for a meal, and I feel again that I'm moving between worlds. The bellboys wear traditional costumes from the days of the Raj, and the tables are draped in starched white linen.

On a more pedestrian note, I am going through mounds of Odomos mosquito repellent. It comes in a tube like toothpaste, and the other day I reached for it in the semi-darkness as I brushed my teeth before Mass. That's not a mistake I'll make twice.

THE MOTHER TERESA EFFECT

My friend kept asking to borrow my dress. I had it dry-cleaned, put a ribbon around it, and slipped the parcel into her room.

ELENA, OXFORDSHIRE

We're all so busy today, one of the most precious things we can offer someone else is our time. And if you do, jump all in: no nodding absentmindedly while you text or eye your screen.   MEGAN, HOBART

Wednesday, January 15, 1997

Kalighat might sound depressing as a hospice, but the volunteers choose to be there and fuel its uplifting spirit. Occasionally, if someone has been there a little too long, their gestures or mood will suggest they have begun to view this work as a job like any other. Otherwise, the atmosphere is buoyant, with an emphasis on teamwork. You might find yourself paired with a volunteer from Greece, Japan, or Russia, and while English is the main foreign tongue, we also make do with body language to get the job done.

THE MOTHER TERESA EFFECT

Leave some coins in your apartment's laundry room. Keep a few stamps in your wallet, as there's always someone who needs one.

DIERK, SAN FRANCISCO

I live downtown near a major hospital. Most weeks, I see a nurse lining up for coffee as I leave. I slip them an envelope with a note and five dollars. I thank them for the work they do, and the difference they make.   OLIVIA, MONTREAL

Monday, January 20, 1997
Tim Tams!

Today an Australian woman arrives at Kalighat. I hear her before I see her, and I close my eyes for a moment to drink in this voice from home. We chat for a few minutes, and she produces two packets of Tim Tam chocolate cookies, an Australian favorite (all college students know the ritual of eating Tim Tams in their jim-jams—or pajamas—when they pull an all-nighter).

How lovely of her, I think, she's brought them to share! Not quite. She is selling them—for twenty dollars per cookie. She softens the shock by saying the money will finance her volunteer time, and I buy two of them. To make it worse, I feel compelled to share them with someone else. Bloody Catholic guilt. (I know, I know. There's a sacrament to absolve guilt, but I'm not sure it applies to hoarding two cookies.)

After my shift, I head to a store called the Good Companion for gift ideas. This outlet supports women from the villages of West Bengal by selling their hand-embroidered linens, from tablecloths to sheets and napkins. It is staffed by volunteers.

The residents at the convent are driving me a little crazy. I listen as long as I can to their squabbles, making sympathetic noises, but sometimes I have to call time out.

THE MOTHER TERESA EFFECT

I grew my hair and donated it to Locks of Love (locksoflove.org) for cancer patients.　　　　　　　　　　JING WEI, LOS ANGELES

While serving food to the homeless, I noticed someone was reading the same book I was. I was startled and ashamed to realize I didn't think of homeless people as readers. I asked her opinion of the book. She smiled and remarked that it was a bit disjointed, unlike the author's other titles. I later sought her and her husband out and admitted my first impression. She smiled graciously and replied, "Who more than

a homeless person needs to be distracted from their current situation?"
She said there were gatherings about once a week under the bridge at
Main Street where they would build a fire in a barrel, exchange stories,
and trade books. I frequently drop off a box of paperbacks under the
bridge, along with reading glasses from the dollar store. The books are
always taken. KATHY, HOUSTON

Tuesday, January 21, 1997

A disturbing trend is surfacing among the male patients at Kalighat: they tie string around their nondominant hand, tighter and tighter each day, to see when it will wither and die. The staff cut it each day, and each night it reappears. "Something to do" is their astonishing explanation. I hear this from several male volunteers, as women look after women and men look after men, by and large.

I understand that most are too weak to go out even briefly, but surely something can be done? Could someone play music once or twice a week? Even a speaker now and then would be good, someone to tell stories and generally amuse. What if a local volunteer simply read from a newspaper in the morning and evening, or a radio played?

∝⟩

I come down with a fever suddenly, and Tess bundles me into a cab and takes me home. It spikes quickly, and they think it's malaria. I feel as though I'm cooking from the inside out. Auntie Grace comes up to see me. I'm especially touched because I know she finds the stairs difficult to manage. She holds a cool compress on my brow and says gently, "It's a chance to be a mother for a moment, yes?" I love her. I have a blood test and insist that they unwrap the fresh needle in front of me.* The test costs $1.50—and that includes express results! Thankfully, it turns out not to be malaria.

---

* I would repeat this years later in a crumbling clinic in Moscow with a sticky floor, where all staff at the news station were sent for HIV tests.

As I lie in bed, I have too much time to think. The isolation stings at times. Then a card or letter arrives, and it fortifies me.

I hope to be better in a day or so. I plan to meet Tess and another volunteer, Judy, for lunch between shifts tomorrow.

THE MOTHER TERESA EFFECT

Forgiveness—of myself. I had been carrying something for ages. Then I heard her talk on self-compassion and knew it wasn't helping anyone to keep carrying this pain.   DR. K., LIVERPOOL

My neighbor volunteers at a poor school, and it broke her heart to see the way the kids dived into the lunch the school provided. She's on a limited income herself, but after talking with a teacher, she supplies a backpack of groceries and a cooked meal each Friday afternoon for a student. The teacher awards it as a "mystery prize" for good behavior, to retain the student's dignity.   CAROLA, LIMA

Wednesday, January 22, 1997

I have to cancel lunch.

After the breakfast dishes are done at Kalighat, I head to the crematorium with a male volunteer. Women reportedly are not encouraged to go to the funeral pyres, but somehow I'm permitted.

Bodies from Kalighat are usually considered unclaimed, so they're laid out and burned as a low priority at the public furnace. It's a much quieter place than the other mortuaries in town. There is no one hawking inflated VIP cremation packages for a parent or grandparent, laced with extra prayers and songs. There is also no service to fast-track you through the meandering lines. A battered, fading sign says an electric cremation takes forty-five minutes, whereas a standard cremation takes four and a half hours.

During the break, a volunteer shares this experience:

We took a body from the van and gently moved it to the pile; what happened next is seared into my DNA. As we lowered the body next to another, the second one . . . moved. We both screamed and jerked back, then we cringed as we were in such a reverent place. The second body wasn't wrapped in white sheets as Kalighat patients are, but rather in an old blanket or thin matted rug.

We quickly moved the body we'd delivered and stared at the one that startled us. Was it some sort of post-mortem reflex? Neither of us had a scrap of medical knowledge. I gingerly played at the edges of the material, and fear turned to panic that whoever was in there was not actually dead. We unwrapped the head and saw the face of an old man, deep lines etched into his withered face. His eyes were closed.

We carried him back to the van and placed him gingerly inside. We were silent for the return ride.

The sister was incredulous. "You brought one back?" she said. She unwrapped him, enlisting the volunteer closest to her. I was moved by the graceful way she handled both the man and his admission into Kalighat: he was to be listed like any other patient brought off the street, as she didn't want him stigmatized. He was carried into the men's area and lasted only a few days more.

❦

I arrive back at the convent to the news Auntie Grace has been taken to hospital, where she is diagnosed with severe osteoporosis and osteo-arthritis. They will keep her in for a few days while the doctors run further tests. She is resting.

A sister offers to take me there, and we hop into a cab. The hospital lobby is utterly packed, several hundred visitors squeezed against each other. We look like cattle herded together in a pen. There is a ticketing system to manage the crush of people, though we see no evidence of it working. The sister moves to the front. "Who are you with?" the guard asks. She holds up the crucifix around her neck. "Him," she declares and marches off. I scurry after her before the startled man can stop us.

Auntie Grace, already so small, looks pale and doll-like in the big hospital bed. We want to take her home where she'll surely get more rest, but the doctors are adamant that she stay overnight.

THE MOTHER TERESA EFFECT

Her lesson to me was to give without fanfare. I imagine when she got started, she didn't have some grand opening day for her first home. No ribbon cutting, no balloons, and no big speeches from dignitaries. She just did it.   CAMERON, GLASGOW

My roommate inherited a gold ring when her Oma (grandma) passed away. She planned to have it melted down and reset into something more modern. I know she was keen to do it, because we'd sketch designs between classes. Instead, she sold it and gave the money to a teenager she knew who was heavily pregnant and scared. It was enough to create a small emergency fund for this new baby.   WINNIE, LONDON

Thursday, January 23, 1997

A friend, Jacquie Mackay, is a morning-show presenter with ABC radio in Queensland, Australia. She calls, and we enjoy a catch-up chat before she interviews me for her program.

I do laundry and get organized ahead of being picked up Saturday by Rita's driver. I want to collect Grace from the hospital, but the sisters have already organized it. I need to remember that they, too, are her family.

There is a delivery from a fax center around the corner. The staff can't make out the name on the cover sheet, so the delivery man simply asks for the foreign girl. It's a message from an old school friend, wishing me safe travels for the next part of my trip.

I then receive a call from ABC radio in Perth—the Peter Kennedy Morning Show. We'll do a prerecorded interview tomorrow at 9:00 A.M. for broadcast next week.

In the late afternoon, I enjoy a lovely chat with Sister Rohita, a doctor based in a town outside Calcutta. She tells me of a twelve-year-old boy who is supporting his family of six. Two mentally disabled siblings are cared for at a home run by the Missionaries of Charity. When the nuns first met him, he was working at a tea garden for forty cents a day. Instead, the sisters helped him set up his own tea shop at the hospital they run. He attends lessons one hour each afternoon, a fact that gives his mother great pride; her son is learning to read and write. They also take him around town to learn how storekeepers display their merchandise. He is doing well. His family now has a stable income—and hope for the future. The nuns don't preach their faith; they live it.

Auntie Grace has been discharged from the hospital and is relishing being back home. I check on her, and I'm pleasantly surprised to find her in a chatty mood.

She reminisces about her childhood and shares that she felt her religious calling at her First Communion. (She believes that God feels such joy when children receive this sacrament, He grants them a wish that day. She recalls telling my eldest sister when she made her First Communion, at age seven or eight, "Pray that Mommy and Daddy always stay together." And half a century later, they have.)

As the years passed and the vocation remained, her aunt Jess took her abroad (a significant luxury at that time) to "get it out of her system." It surprises me to hear this. My grandmother was a woman of deep faith, and I'd assumed this applied to the family as a whole, or at least that they would support a call to religious life. Maybe I underestimated the lure of grandchildren!

On a more somber note, Grace shares a story that underscored her commitment to becoming a nun. She grew up as the only girl in a gaggle of rambunctious boys (my father among them); an aunt and uncle would take her out now and then to make her feel special. (As at Kalighat, "aunt" and "uncle" are often used as titles of respect for those not related.) One particular day, they treated her to a picnic on the shores of a lake. To Grace's everlasting regret, she suggested a swim and wasted no time jumping into the water. Her enthusiasm was no match for her water skills, and she soon found herself out of her depth, literally and figuratively. She was frantic.

The uncle jumped in to rescue her, but soon struck trouble as well. His wife, who had been sunning herself on a rock, leaped into action, but to no avail. After thrashing about to the point of exhaustion, he was swallowed by the water right in front of them. He had been a prominent magistrate, and the newspaper covered his death. It reported that a local fisherman found his body, and doctors concluded he had suffocated on his partial dentures.

Grace never quite came to terms with the loss of his life in an effort to save her own. Decades later, it was clear the pain had not entirely subsided. Soon after the incident, she developed a compulsion to wash her hands that would stay with her through her life. "Serving others is the very least I can do for penance," she says quietly.

THE MOTHER TERESA EFFECT

I respect that the only value she saw in her fame was to encourage more people to help the poor. In an age when people would rather go viral than go out and help others, she stands out. JAMILA, QATAR

In the month of May (which is devoted to the Virgin Mary), we pray the rosary each night as a family. MATEO, OAKLAND

Friday, January 24, 1997

I'll head to Rita's home tomorrow, and from there, we'll leave for the airport for my flight to the country.

There was a call for me—Charmaine, a friend and former social-work colleague, had phoned. It's so thoughtful of her.

∝≺⟩

I try to call her back, but no one answers.

I then phone another friend, Angela, to thank her for her stream of letters. She answers and almost falls off her chair in shock. The connection is poor (it sounds as though she's at the bottom of a well), but it's lovely to hear her voice.

I use a typewriter today for the first time since Ms. Kinsey's ninth-grade typing class. It's a German model, seemingly from an era of steam trains and ladies' bonnets. It's full of symbols I don't know and seems to be missing the vital ones I need.

It's my last full day here, so it's time to take a few more photos of the sisters around the grounds.*

The sisters read widely, play music, and enjoy movies. But tonight they entertain themselves by offering to dress me in one of their habits. First a slip, then the dress itself, followed by the veil, and finally a crucifix on a chain. They laugh like schoolgirls as they dream up my religious name: Sister Sweet Tooth. Sister Talks-Too-Fast. Sister Walks-Too-Fast. They nail them all. Clearly, I have not learned their meditative pace.

They had seen *Sister Act* with Whoopi Goldberg and thought it was hysterical. I think of Jon, who had worried that I would go to India and somehow come back a nun, just like that. I'm tempted to wear the habit when he picks me up at the airport, to give him a heart attack. I hesitate only because I'm not sure I could pass as a nun; I have a navel ring. It has already sent off a few rickety airport alarms in India, after which I found myself surrounded by female staff who poked at it and gasped at each other. This, in an entire country of pierced noses.

I wear my habit to surprise Auntie Grace. She laughs, then looks pensive; it seems to remind her of something. She asks me to sit down, and I wonder what's on her mind. "Child," she begins, "you know we love Jon . . ."

I'm puzzled. "Yes, Auntie?"

"But a calling to God supersedes everything."

I'm taken aback. Is she honestly suggesting an annulment?

"Auntie, I look good in black, but is that enough reason be a nun?"

"Child," she says again, smiling and sighing. I do love to exasperate her. I am so touched, but I can't seriously continue this conversation. She's unwell and tired, and I can't strain her further with a fruitless debate.

---

* When the snapshots are developed, the nuns radiate joy, as if lit from within. I had noticed this already—I believe anyone would—but I am delighted to see it captured on film.

"Okay," I say, "I'll do it, but I want to be fast-tracked. If it takes seven years to be a nun, I want to get there in three."

"It doesn't work like that," she says, with such sincerity I want to hug her. I squeeze her hand. "I guess it's not for me, then."

And just like that, my one-minute career as a sister is dashed.

THE MOTHER TERESA EFFECT

I let people cut in line. Not every day, but often. It costs you minutes, but it sends a message: it's not all about me. I'm happy to help you ease your day, in however small a way. BLAKE, PHILADELPHIA

I'll admit it: I was kind of a jealous person. I would resent people's successes, wealthy parents, car, you name it. Then my college RA (residential advisor) said, "If you're going to be jealous of someone's life, you've got to be jealous of their whole *life, not just the parts you want for yourself." That stuck in my head.* CARMEN, LOS ANGELES

Saturday, January 25, 1997

At Kalighat, a man is deteriorating rapidly, and he is moved to a bed near the front for closer monitoring. I think back to the man rescued from the funeral pyre, who passed away at Kalighat without ever regaining consciousness. Had he been in some sort of a coma? Did someone discover him on the street, genuinely think he was dead, and do what they felt was the right thing? I'd like to think it was the work of a misguided good Samaritan rather than someone who wanted him removed from the sidewalk outside a store.

I say goodbye to the patients, the sisters, and the other volunteers. I have loved my time here, and I've been so moved by the compassion and kindness I have witnessed. I don't mind being the cliché who cries as she leaves.

There's a tearful goodbye at the convent as I get organized for my stay at the rural hospital. The other residents, while quietly driving me mad, have never stopped being caring. And, of course, the sisters have been so gracious and so welcoming.

THE MOTHER TERESA EFFECT

I didn't expect her to inspire me in my business goals, but she did. She had this single-minded clarity and determination that applies to so much in life.　　　　　　　　　　　　　　　　　NOLA, GALWAY

My cousin cheated me out of some money, and I cut him off, and his child too. I realized I was punishing my niece out of anger toward her father. I still no longer speak to my cousin, but I see his child.

STEPHEN, BRIGHTON

—*//*—

PART IV

The Leprosy Ward

HEADING TO THE COUNTRY

Sunday, January 26, 1997

It's Australia Day at home, and I think of everyone enjoying the holiday weekend and the traditional evening fireworks over the Swan River.

Time to leave Calcutta and head to the leprosy ward in the country.

(Prior to coming here, I had visited a travel clinic to ensure my vaccinations were up to date. I asked the doctor about whether I needed anything special for the leprosy ward, beyond the recommended typhoid, hepatitis B, and tetanus shots. He said it would be enough to continue with regular hygiene, as my immune system is strong, and I'd be having limited contact with open wounds. By contrast, the patients themselves are severely malnourished—the new arrivals, at least—and their immune systems are ragged, unable to mount a defense.)

Rita takes me to the airport, but we're not sure the flight will even take off; the airline workers have been on strike for two days.

It's a bumpy but bearable flight. As we touch down, everyone claps. I find this unnerving; it implies they weren't ever sure the pilot would get us there safely in the first place.

I'm excited for this next chapter of the trip, but I grow quiet as I turn a corner in the Bagdogra airport and find myself walking through the arrivals section behind a coffin. A young police officer had died in a train accident that very morning. About sixty men surround the casket as it arrives. As the crowd disperses, I find the nuns from the rural hospital there to greet me, and their warmth resonates immediately.

On the way back, we see a man riding along on a bicycle with over fifty chicken carcasses attached, their plumes waving in the wind. I stop to drink in this theater, then hurry to catch up with the others as they walk to the van.

By the time I get to my room, it's dusk.

Good news: The shower in the bathroom actually has a shower fitted. Less than good news: there is no hot water, and it's freezing outside.

As the sisters leave my room, one pauses at the threshold to warn me of several dogs on the property that are believed to be rabid. She'll fill me in tomorrow, she says.

THE MOTHER TERESA EFFECT

I watched a documentary on her, and I was struck by the energy she maintained through her seventies and eighties. I realized we have the same twenty-four hours in the day—how much was I squandering on mindless things? MADDIE, JOHANNESBURG

Actually, she inspired me to wear less makeup. I was applying more and more as the years went by. I'd see her photo and I'd think, Well, of course she's barefaced, she's a nun. But there was more to it. She was showing the world her natural self, unafraid. Meanwhile, my makeup was becoming a mask to hide behind. I still wear it, but much less. VIOLETTA, MADRID

Monday, January 27, 1997

I'm shown around the hospital campus, comprising a general ward, a tuberculosis ward, and the leprosy ward where I'll be based. The three units are joined by dirt paths, and a long driveway sprouts from the public road to the main buildings. The nearest phone is two miles from here at a parish center; I can receive calls from Jon there.

A sister hands me a white coat and shows me how to log medication. I look like one of those fake doctors in pharmaceutical ads at home, and laugh to think what Jon would make of this.

I'm shadowing a paramedic who oversees the ward. I join him on his rounds of the hundred or so patients. He writes in the medical file, and I copy the same onto a second register, divided into lists of x-rays, operations, and other information. I'll see a procedure done tomorrow—a "BKA," or below-the-knee amputation.

I'm writing at my desk by candlelight. We've had a few blackouts already, and you never know how long they'll last. It reminds me of the convent in Calcutta where they turn off "the current" and the water for long periods of time to save money.

THE MOTHER TERESA EFFECT

Our daughter's classmate was trying to keep up her grades while her parents went through a bitter divorce. We took a deep breath and invited her to live with us for the final semester before graduation. She says that having a neutral place made all the difference. JAN, BUTTE

My grandmother lived with us, and I recall each night she would sit in her rocking chair, reciting the rosary until I thought the beads would wear down. She said she prayed for all the family and did a special decade (round of prayers) for Mother Teresa. When the nun died, I asked who'd receive her final prayers now. "Still Mother Teresa," she said. "Now I'm praying to her, not for her." TIM, CALGARY

A LESSON I'LL NEVER FORGET

Tuesday, January 28, 1997

I miss Auntie Grace. Back in Calcutta, it's her feast day (that is, the feast day of Saint Thomas Aquinas, who inspired her religious name). She's still unwell and growing more frail, but I know the sisters take wonderful and loving care of her. My heart squeezes to think that when I get back to Calcutta, I'll see my aunt for the final time.

Though I don't know it yet, today I'll learn a lesson in determination and overcoming adversity that will stay with me always.

Adit, a patient in his late thirties, is scheduled for a below-the-knee amputation. He is a longtime leprosy sufferer and now his entire calf is an open wound of rotting flesh. His body uses every ounce of strength it possesses to fight this disease. While it might sound dire, an amputation would give the rest of his body a chance to heal.

The operating room is threadbare, and Adit squirms, his eyes wide and fearful. I am positioned near him, and my "job," if you can call it that, is to stroke his hair and shoulders until he loses consciousness. I'm unsure whether he wants it, but I gently stroke his arm and watch for a reaction. He turns away but smiles faintly and nods a silent "acha," so I keep going.

A doctor arrives and administers a general anesthetic, then leaves. As he walks out the door, he instructs me that if the patient begins to stir, I am to sit on his chest if need be—to keep him from seeing anything. *What does that mean? Won't they use enough anesthesia to keep him under?* I shoot the staff a quizzical look, but they smile and nod in reassurance; two others are already set to work.

I watch the initial incision, fascinated as they peel away layer after layer of flesh at the base of his knee. All manner of delicate instruments is passed from a metal tray. I'm startled, then, to see a nurse produce a saw. It looks similar to one you'd find in any hardware store back home or in probably half the backyard sheds in the country. I grit my teeth at the sound of the sawing as they detach his lower leg.

The job is almost done, when the anesthesia begins to wear off. They quickly give him an injection of something clear.

Finally, the procedure is complete. The calf is gone, and the upper bone is smoothed and skin stitched over and around it. I am impressed. And I'm about to be impressed even more. The two men take off their gloves, and I'm shocked to see they both have stumps for fingers. I am speechless. They have just performed this work deftly and successfully, without one full hand of fingers between them, and without one hour in medical school.

Later, as he comes to, Adit keeps repeating a phrase over and over. One of the men says it's a side effect of the drugs in the IV drip. He recalls a procedure he performed with a patient recovering in the next room, only a thin curtain separating the two. Not once, but the entire time, the voice wafted over, "I'm going to kill you with my gun. I'm going to kill you with my gun." Moments before the drug had taken effect, the patient had been recalling his time as a soldier in the Indo-Pakistani War of 1971, and then the thought played like a record with the needle stuck. It's exactly what you need when you're trying to operate.

In the early evening, I walk with a sister to run some errands and to send a fax to *The West Australian*, pitching a feature article about Mother Teresa's replacement.

We buy containers of *russagullas*, sweet balls of cheese curd swimming in a heavenly syrup. It's thick, lush, and flavored with cardamom.

Later, I'm saying the rosary alone in the chapel when we have another blackout. At first, I'm a little thrown, but then it occurs to me: *I'm in a chapel—how much safer could I be?*

My thoughts drift in the darkness, and I recall an old adage: *Hide money in a Bible; those who open its pages won't steal, and those who steal won't open its pages.*

When I was in college, some parents sent their daughter off to university with her own copy. When she'd call home to vent about the transition to dorm life or a general lack of money, they'd say things like, "Go to this verse; it will bring you comfort," or "Read this passage; it has the solution you're looking for." Of course, she would say she had read the passages . . . but never did. She graduated before she ever opened the Bible and gasped to find more than a thousand dollars folded among the parables. I guess it adds new meaning to "the riches of the Scripture."

I think about Adit and wonder how he's feeling after his amputation. I look forward to seeing him tomorrow.

THE MOTHER TERESA EFFECT

She let nothing get in her way. I, on the other hand, am a master of procrastination. I finally finished my book.   GEORGE, LUANDA

I write letters that get results, so I volunteer one afternoon a week to help people draft correspondence on anything from airline refunds and land-tax assessments to victim impact statements.
MIRIAM, NEW YORK CITY

Wednesday, January 29, 1997

My scalp itches, and I convince myself I have lice. It's possible, I reason; I spent two hours yesterday bent over the patient. The nurse inspects my scalp but doesn't think so. I'm relieved to find she's right.

I look forward to seeing Adit on the rounds with the paramedic. I'm startled to see the color in his cheeks. He looks tired but otherwise happy and keeps staring at his calf—or rather, where his calf used to be. I wonder if he will feel phantom pains in the future. A crutch leans against his bed, ready to be of service.

This morning I learned how to test for diabetes by detecting sugar in the urine. We use Benedict's solution, eight drops of urine, and an ancient Bunsen burner.

In the afternoon I fold gauze. And fold gauze. And fold gauze. To kill the time, I practice Bengali phrases with some of the patients, and they collapse on the floor in hysterics.

My eyes feel strained; maybe I need to have them tested.

We take dinner by candlelight again, as blackouts strike.

The sisters and brothers run several mobile clinics. One is conducted at a community that has sprouted up around an abandoned railway platform. Another focuses on the red-light district, with efforts to raise awareness of HIV and AIDS among the prostitutes. Yet a third is for leprosy patients on the outskirts of town. I hope to assist at each of these outreach services.

In the evening, Brother Benito walks with me in the dark to the local church. We have dinner with the nuns and a priest—a real character who loves to tease and needle. I enjoy a lovely call from Jon while we're there. He had recently gone to the Australia Day fireworks show with friends, Charmaine and Mike, and they had packed a picnic for him. They have been wonderful, helping to keep him busy.

I chat with two deacons (priests in training) at the gate before turning in.

As I head to sleep, I feel a wall of quilts engulfing me. I think of the fairy tale "The Princess and the Pea," except I'm the pea under all this weight.

THE MOTHER TERESA EFFECT

She inspired me to look more closely at a career in nursing. She was old, yet her eyes shone. Why? Because she loved what she did. It took two years to align my life more with my values, but I'll graduate nursing next year.　　　　　　　　　　　　　　ALAN, LOS ANGELES

I gave someone a second chance, when I had vowed to write him off.
　　　　　　　　　　　　　　　　　　　　　　BILL, HOBART

Thursday, January 30, 1997

We all get a lecture from the priest after morning Mass; he says we're vacating the front pews and that it's insulting. I bite my lip so as not to laugh; it seems parishioners do this around the world.

I miss my exercise, so I walk up and down the driveway for forty-five minutes after lunch to stretch my legs. I've tried the roads but they're dangerous, as trucks tear by, blasting their horns and belching black clouds of pollution. And it's tiring to fend off repeated offers of a ride from rickshaw drivers or street vendors who want to sell me snacks, water, or knickknacks. The other day I was offered a variety of dead beetles mounted on a strip of cardboard, ripped from the top of a cookie box. You have to admire their resourcefulness.

People are very curious and talk among themselves as I pace back and forth. It seems novel for them. I soon forget, lost in thought and composing my next letter in my head. I replay a conversation with the nuns on mindfulness, so I jolt back to the present.

Back on the ward, I'm handed tweezers and shown how to remove maggots from wounds. One man appears to have a moving white blanket across his leg. Maggot therapy, I'm told, is useful to a degree, as they eat the rotting flesh. At some point, though, these fly larvae need to be removed. Two staff members are bickering gently, one insisting the therapy is dated, and the other vowing it's a classic treatment.

More blackouts.

THE MOTHER TERESA EFFECT

Instead of the whole holiday hoopla, our family pools gift money for the adults and donates it to clean-water projects in Africa.

MAUREEN, SPOKANE

Our priest asked if we could help a family who had fallen on especially hard times. The father had a job, but it paid little, and they kept moving to ever-cheaper rentals. The mother stayed home, as their child had special needs and found any change distressing. My wife and I looked at each other and went home to crunch numbers. Yes, we could help with the rent, but that was a band-aid. We lent them a home deposit so they could get a mortgage at less than their current rent.

A. AND S., CAMBRIDGE

Friday, January 31, 1997

More gauze.

Staff use plaster of Paris to set a cast for a female patient. After the rounds, I do some reading on the signs and social stigma of leprosy.

I notice that some of the long-term patients have flattened noses; a nun explains that a collapsed nasal bridge is common in leprosy sufferers, as the disease affects the extremities. The paramedic adds that leprosy and tuberculosis look surprisingly similar under the microscope: one is bacterial and one is viral.

Leprosy sufferers often won't or can't care for themselves at home or on the street. Some rip off bandages and let flies settle on the wounds—how else to beg coins for their children? A clean dressing won't help someone desperate for basic survival.

Some of the children at the hospital have delayed milestones. There is a boy here who looks to be around age ten; I am shocked to learn he is sixteen. And when I first saw Chandni, a daughter of one of the leprosy patients, I assumed she was about two years old; in fact, she is five. She is plainly adored, and yet she seems to have that rag-doll quality or "floppy baby syndrome" one associates with neglected children. Staff say she has weak muscle growth and delayed milestones, and a near-total lack of stimuli.

On a lighter note, children here seem more innocent, with inquisitive, rich imaginations not dulled by computer games. They also seem content to be children, rather than in a hurry to grow up.

I'm torn. I miss Jon terribly, but I'm not quite ready to leave.

On the hospital grounds is a small central pond area with a hand pump. Men bathe here, while women wash pots and pans a few feet away. What might have been a merely decorative water feature in the West takes on a much more practical purpose. I join the patients in watering the garden by hand.

On February 7 and 9, the staff will split into two groups, taking turns for an annual picnic.

A random observation:

Indian bras are appalling. They mainly consist of two triangles of material held together with elastic and hope. Add to this, the little stalls where they're sold are almost invariably run by men, so the women hurriedly choose something and flee. I had seen the same types of bras in Calcutta stores, and now again fluttering on the clothesline. Grown women have to make do with these.

THREE DOGS

I AM WALKING BACK FROM the leprosy ward to my room when I hear dogs behind me, barking and snapping. I assume they are the rabid mutts that the sisters had warned me about. My knees go to water. I have a flashback to age six, when a German shepherd got excited by my swinging schoolbag and jumped up on me, putting a paw on each of my shoulders. There I froze, his snout and my nose inches apart.

I am shocked at what comes out of my mouth: I hear myself say, "Thank you, God, for protecting me." Not *please*, or *would you*, or *could you*, but giving thanks in advance. The instant I say it, the dogs stop barking and snarling. They trot beside me for a moment before losing interest.

I take a moment to absorb this. Eventually I feel my legs return to normal and run to tell the sisters. One shares a similar story: she knew a woman, a friend of her mother's, who was picked up by an elephant. She quickly shouted, "In the name of God, put me down." And it did so, immediately.

At Kalighat volunteers are called "auntie" or "uncle." Here I'm called "sister," and I give up trying to correct them.

The patients are making "coal balls" for the fire from a mixture of cow dung and *kanjee* water (the starchy liquid left over when rice is rinsed). They dip, roll, and stack deftly, some with only stumps for fingers or hands.

In the afternoon I take my walk along the driveway. More people come to watch, amused. One or two bring folding chairs! I hear a woman say, "This girl walks and walks, and she goes nowhere!" It reminds me of Rita's words when we first arrived: "Indians almost glide along."

A letter arrives from friends with news from home, and they thoughtfully include some pages torn from a gossip magazine.

I finish off the day with stockpiling more folded gauze.

I hope to go to Siliguri, a nearby town, tomorrow with Sister Agatha. The weather is very cool.

THE MOTHER TERESA EFFECT

Way before she was famous, Mother Teresa was just Agnes. She believed in herself, and look where she ended up.   CARLITA, AGE 11, OAKLAND

I live in an apartment building, and I mostly keep a friendly distance with the others. Don't get involved, you know? Then Masha (a Russian nickname for Maria) moved in, and she kept smiling and waving. She is a struggling single mom, and yet she was always cheery, checking on someone from temple or offering a friendly cup of coffee. I began to smile back more, and I've gotten to know her. She's made me reconsider the meaning of community.   BLAKE, MELBOURNE

Sunday, February 2, 1997

Mass today at the parish center. A few of us walk; others take the rickety bus and complain about how poorly the system is run.

Two of the female staff, cheerful older teenagers, are leaving for town this morning, and the sisters will collect them later. They talk excitedly about the day they have planned.

The sun comes out in the afternoon after a very bleak morning.

My eyes are acting up. I saw flickering light for the third time. At first it seemed inside my right eye, and then twice on the walls of the room.

I hop in an auto-ric with Sister Agatha, and we head out of the gates. She is in her mid-eighties but gave up driving only last year. She sustains a withering pace as she oversees the hospital.

The outdoor markets are colorful and bustling. Vegetables are spread out on sheets in the dirt. Cuffed bags of spices are also laid out, forming a patchwork quilt of orange (turmeric), black (mustard seeds), and other hues.

We visit the "cripple house" (What can I say? They call a spade a spade.) and a community facility called Rankwell Village. Sister Agatha says it was founded by Austrian visitors two years ago. She recalls with a smile that skeptics were sure the crucifix and flag would be long gone, but they still stand proudly.

Later, the house girls dress me up in a sari and top it off with a *bindi* ("BIN-thee"), an adhesive decorative piece between my eyes. They laugh and gossip as they play stylists.

Lawrence, one of the religious brothers, offers to walk me to the church tonight so I can receive a call from Jon. We'll be back in time for rosary.

Jon is feeling down. He is still living at the boys' boarding school as a housemaster's assistant, and they're having trouble with some "rent-a-poms," English students who come for a semester to help. They're noisy and more interested in partying than showing up for their shifts to oversee the students. It's becoming draining. ("Poms" is slang for British people who came to Australia. The word has various origins; one popular theory refers to the early convicts who arrived as "Prisoners of Mother England." POME became POM somewhere along the line.)

He says my radio interview was played several times. The chaplain at the school where we live is considering volunteering in India too. Jon will begin lecturing four hours a week at a local college in addition to his regular job. I'm proud of him.

I hear his voice and it's so clear, I feel I can reach out and touch him.

THE MOTHER TERESA EFFECT

Mom says Mother Teresa had to fight for people to give her a chance. I get that.   TOM, AGE 14, PORTLAND

I pray in the car. It feels like the only time I get to myself. GINA, ROME

Monday, February 3, 1997

Today is the feast of Saint Blaise (aka Blase)—the patron saint of sore throats. I'm familiar with a range of saints (I'd forked over my allowance often enough to Saint Anthony of Padua, patron of lost things, over library books and favorite tops), but I've never heard of something so specific. Sister Mala is slightly horrified at my ignorance. Earlier she'd made a comment on Don Bosco that I half heard. "No, I don't think I've met him," I offered. Probably not, I realized later, given he'd died centuries ago. She had been too gracious to correct me. Somewhere, my religion teacher is turning in her grave.

THE RAILWAY CLINIC

I JOIN SISTER IRENE FOR A mobile clinic at the abandoned railway station in Siliguri. By "clinic" I mean a small folding table, two folding chairs, and a stool for the patient, all of which we carry there. Our "medicine kit" consists of several plastic bags of supplies, carried on the half-hour bus journey. We pass a few tiny towns, the largest with stores and a tea garden. Many shops have no way for the customers to enter; you simply talk to the owner over a counter and they reach behind for whatever you point at. This might be anything from individual cigarettes to tiny pairs of aspirin packaged in cellophane.

Hundreds of people live in, under, and around the abandoned platform. Everywhere, there are makeshift tents made of discarded grocery bags or canvas squares, whatever can be salvaged. Plastic sheets are sewn together to form walls, and cardboard is propped up optimistically to little effect. The squalor is rancid, and the children are filthy and malnourished. Little ones play with rats. I'm a bit startled to see once-wild boar roaming around, sniffing out any scraps of food that a human has missed.

Yet among this misery is a sense of community. The inhabitants are knitted together in abject poverty, supporting one another as they try to eke out an existence. Even as the occasional fight breaks out, there is an overriding generosity of spirit and altruism among them. Food is shared and compassion is abundant in a setting where it would be easy to grow angry and bitter.

Lita, a staff member from the hospital, is with us to interpret, but everyone presses forward, a wall of arms, sores, and wounds. Gorgeous babies are covered in scabies and weeping sores. People form a line, but it dissolves within moments. The concept of queuing seems foreign and unnecessary to them. I think how much more useful I would be if I were a nurse. All I can do is clean and dress wounds as best I know, give eardrops, administer cough syrup, and other basic things such as fever medication or eye ointment.

Sister Irene tends to anything more complicated. I see young teenage mothers with malnourished babies. It is heartbreaking.

Time flies and before we know it, it's time to head back. We "splurge" forty rupees (less than a dollar) on an auto-ric home to save time, rather than contend with a bus for a few pennies.

❧

People here don't hesitate to ask for sponsors—someone to send them money every month—and who can blame them? I met a woman for two minutes when she asked if I could organize sponsors for her sons. A little boy sidled up to request the same thing. In Calcutta, a woman had insisted on writing down her name and details while we waited for a tram. I was also approached at the Bagdogra airport.

There is another blackout, and we eat by candlelight. I recall a friend telling me about a trendy restaurant in Europe where customers dine in pitch black and all the wait staff are blind. We're all swaddled in coats, gloves, and scarves to fight the cold.

THE MOTHER TERESA EFFECT

I work in a pretty toxic environment. She reminds me to show compassion to those who least deserve it.   LORRAINE, WASHINGTON, DC

I coach junior athletics. There was this kid, not a great performer but the perfect attitude about sports and sportsmanship. I noticed his parents never came to watch him. It bugged me, but I found out later that they both worked two jobs. When the boy won a regional trophy, I threw a pizza party for him at the clubhouse, and we toasted with soda. That was years ago, but I still choke up to think how proud he looked.   MERVIN, OAKLAND

Tuesday, February 4, 1997

I'm twenty-nine! The last year of my twenties before the more conservative thirties? Are elasticized pants and rhinestone sweaters in my future? Shoot me now.

An absolutely fantastic day!

In the morning, I happily fetch and carry while staff conduct some minor procedures, debriding (smoothing) calluses and removing stitches.

Lunchtime is mail time, and I have a letter from Angela. She has made an astounding effort. Every week, correspondence arrives from her.

I walk with the brothers to the parish center to receive a call. The gate is locked, and we have to jump a wall. There are shards of glass—perhaps an attempted break-in? No one's really sure.

After dinner, I'm surprised with not one but *three* birthday calls! It's lovely to hear Jon's voice, but he sounds despondent, as the situation with the rent-a-poms has worsened. He blasted them, and the whole boarding house heard—then the housemaster followed suit. They were reeling by the end of it.

In an age of video, it's amazing how much can be conveyed in a voice. Our nieces and nephews sing me happy birthday, which is very sweet.

THE MOTHER TERESA EFFECT

I travel frequently for work and was racking up the dollars on snacks and magazines at the airport. Our parish newsletter had an article on her. Now I subscribe to the magazines (way cheaper!) and have directed the difference to a local women's shelter.

ANNALEISE, HARTFORD

Every office has one: the person who shoots down ideas, resists change, and won't work a minute of overtime. Ours was part of the furniture, and I resented being assigned a project with her. Then I headed in early one day ahead of the deadline, and was shocked to see her across the road, handing out sandwiches to the homeless near the subway. I made sure to treat her better after that. MIKE, NEW YORK CITY

Wednesday, February 5, 1997

We begin the day with Mass at a neighboring chapel; everyone is very warm and welcoming.

It's Sister Agatha's feast day, and we sing the song I now know by heart.

I'm delighted to head back to the railway clinic with Sister Irene and Lita—I really enjoy it.

Among the patients, a six-year-old boy shyly presents his two-year-old brother for his sores to be cleaned. I wish I could bundle them up and transfer them to a happy childhood with full tummies, where their only worry might be an occasional scratch from climbing trees. The older brother is endearingly gentle with the younger one. When it's his own turn, I realize more fully how shy he really is, and I'm touched that he overcame it earlier to ensure his little brother was seen. Adults flip their children from side to side to quickly show the range of wounds, boils, and abrasions.

THE MOTHER TERESA EFFECT

Service to others is a privilege, not a chore. That's what I think of when I see her picture.   JOAN, MONTGOMERY

I craved a new direction. My passions? Live performance and conjuring vivid imagery through storytelling. I told God to send me a sign. Within a week, someone sent me an email "by accident" for sightintosound .org. Through my association with them, I've read for the blind and those with reading difficulties like dyslexia. I'll soon be accompanying the visually impaired to the ballet or opera, to describe in detail what's going on.   L., HOUSTON

DARJEELING

Thursday, February 6, 1997

I head to Darjeeling with Sister Irene and her friend Cate, visiting from Britain. Malika, one of the staff, also comes along. We hire a minivan for less than fifteen dollars, gas included.

Stunning views of the majestic Himalayan mountain range and the town of Kurseong ("CURSE-ee-yong") unfold. We take in tea plantations and tiny stores draped in marigold garlands. The scenery is a welcome distraction, as I don't want to think how fast the driver is taking the hairpin bends.

The wind is icy as we drop off Cate at a convent. I wash my hands, and the water is so cold it feels at first as though it's burning. The fuel is rationed, so the heaters are rarely on.

Malika disappears to visit friends in the area. Sister Irene and I have lunch at a little restaurant. We order roast chicken—and we're served half a chicken each. The servings are strikingly large compared to those at the hospital. We look at each other, and Sister Irene resolves it with a swirl of her finger. She signals the waiter to box up one of them and to give it to a blind man and his son, who are begging outside.

At the cash register, I'm startled to meet a man from my hometown.

On the journey down, we stop at a convent in Kurseong, and are welcomed into a blissfully warm kitchen. Two sisters dance around the stove in glee, and I smile at the joy they take in simple pleasures. Auntie Grace was based here for many years as a Mother Superior and a school principal. I am shown her old room, and I imagine her as a younger nun, sorting lesson plans or overseeing meetings. We also tour a delightfully quaint chapel, more than a century old.

There is also a boarding school and a dormitory brimming with rows of beds. Thick blankets are displayed in every color and pattern. Simple hooks adorn the walls for little bathrobes and pajamas. This is the home where, decades earlier, Mother Teresa had sent my aunt the forty orphans she feared she could not feed.

We were up before dawn, and all of us struggle to stay awake at dinner.

THE MOTHER TERESA EFFECT

Look at what she achieved around the world. She had a vision, and she kept up the momentum until she made it a reality. DON, PROVIDENCE

The school was having a bake sale, and I knew another mother had no spare time. I told her I'd do enough for both our kids and dropped off the cake to her home that morning, so her child wouldn't arrive to class empty-handed. HUA, SAN FRANCISCO

Friday, February 7, 1997

Half the employees are out on an annual picnic. The other half will go Sunday. There will be no railway clinic today, as the wards are short-staffed.

Brother Benito is back early from a trip to Nepal, as it was utterly freezing.

The electricity is off again. So is the water. It's frustrating.

At lunch, conversation turns to the customs of the Parsis, an Indian ethnic group of Persian (Iranian) heritage, and the Tower of Silence they use when someone dies. Instead of cremation, the staff explain, the body is placed high on the inner ledges of a tower or silo. Vultures come to devour the corpse, and their job is done within an hour. This really appeals to me as a way to go: clean, fast, and back to nature. Failing that, throw me in a cardboard box.

The first group of picnickers got rained on, but return smiling.

THE MOTHER TERESA EFFECT

You can go through the motions of helping someone, but you add so much more with a side serving of joy. FILIA, LOS ANGELES

Gossip is addictive, just like smoking—and you could say, just as toxic. It took a while, but I cut down bit by bit. ESTHER, MELBOURNE

Saturday, February 8, 1997

I stay on the leprosy ward today, as Cate requests to go instead to the railway clinic.

Things I'm looking forward to at home:
> Seeing Jon.
> Seeing Jon.
> Seeing Jon.
> Seeing my family and Jon's.

> Catching up with friends.
> Sunshine.
> Ice cream at the beach and sausages off the grill (I've avoided most dairy and meat here).
> Getting a real haircut.

THE MOTHER TERESA EFFECT

She reminds me that everyone is equal. I knew this intellectually, but not spiritually. A casual remark made me look around. I was choosing friends, boyfriends, even my car according to what would make me look better. It was hard to admit to myself, but liberating at the same time.

BASHIRA, PHILADELPHIA

Every family celebration comes with a huge buffet meal, and I would think nothing of going back for seconds or even thirds. Then my child had a school assembly on poverty around the world, and I decided to limit my portions in honor of those who go hungry.

MONTY, STOCKHOLM

Sunday, February 9, 1997

I skip the second phase of the annual picnic and go instead to a nearby town, where the sisters run a school and hospital.

I'd been planning to stay overnight and to "assist" (I use the word loosely) on a procedure for a sixteen-year-old with peritonitis, a severe abdominal infection. But one of the sisters is called back unexpectedly, and we need to leave together. Instead, I make plans to fax Radio Australia tomorrow.

Jon is on a field trip to Queensland (in Australia's northeast), but he'll try to call, which is very thoughtful given all he's juggling right now.

Tonight at dinner, the sisters discuss enneagrams, a personality-ranking system with nine numbered types. Most religious members, they tell me, are type six. Apparently that means they're loyal but can't make a decision. I smile, but it feels rude to agree with them. It's sounds true, though; it seems they're taught to think as a group and to defer decisions that affect them intimately.

THE MOTHER TERESA EFFECT

"Read this profile on Mother Teresa," said my roommate, and included the link. It made me look at my own profile—seriously. It got me on a more spiritual path. Fewer selfies, more genuine connection.

KIM, LAS VEGAS

My parents used to volunteer at a soup kitchen and made me go with them from age fifteen. I did it but refused to look at anyone, and prayed no one from school would see me walking in or out. My mother would chat to the men and women, look them in the eye, maybe touch their arm as she cleared their plate. Then it hit me: these people were used to being ignored, abused, even spat on. They came here for something different, and I gave them the same cold shoulder. Things started to change in me that day. JESS, MANCHESTER

Monday, February 10, 1997

After work, I make another attempt to beat the ancient typewriter into submission. It rebels and the ribbon has the audacity to run out of ink halfway through. I scream words likely never heard before in the walls of a convent. I'm sick of the isolation, run-down machinery, and lack of phones on the property. I'm getting fed up with the general inefficiency and unreliability of India.

I get a round-trip auto-ric to fax Radio Australia. After my fruitless typing session, I can send only a handwritten letter, so they might well discard it. Still, it feels like having a ticket in the lottery, and that's enough right now.

We head to the airport to see Cate on her flight back to the UK. The airline staff insist the travel agent undercharged her and demand another 10 percent. She refuses, as she's already paid for her fare in full. I'm interested to watch this pantomime, as I had gone directly to another airline and also paid in full, so who knows what they'll tell me. Given the exchange rate, the additional charge is nothing to lose sleep over; it's simply another example of the way people try to pad out costs.

I pick up Sister Agatha from the convent school. It has 105 students, including upper and lower kindergarten and standards (grades) 1–4. The school is kept afloat by a blend of local and foreign donors.

We head to Siliguri armed with a list of supplies: twenty dozen eggs, a little portable stove, and shoes for some of the leprosy patients (when toes are missing, shoes can help lend balance and traction).

The markets are bustling. Sheets are laid out on the floor to designate a stall, wares are displayed, and men squat as they await customers. Vegetables are fanned out: onions, potatoes, beans. Cows, so thin their ribs protrude, tread through everything; they're never challenged as they're considered holy.

Meat hangs in the open air as flies buzz around it.

⌒✣⌒

Jon has another field trip.

I fly out a week from today! I *cannot wait* to see him.

THE MOTHER TERESA EFFECT

I had slacked off on the volunteering. I signed up again at a hospital.

CISSY, HOUSTON

We hired a gardener we didn't really need, to help him support a grandchild he never expected to raise.

L., ALBERTA

Tuesday, February 11, 1997

There are some minor operations scheduled in the morning. I'm struck by one patient, a man with the kindest face, sweet eyes, and a salt-and-pepper beard. Unfortunately, he also has horrifically infected toes, which are split open and rotting. Decaying flesh truly has its own smell.

Afternoon: I am furious. Sister Agatha has mentioned—*in passing, no less*—that Auntie Grace is back in hospital. For how long?

I had no idea; no one said anything. Too late, they say, to get a seat on tomorrow's plane. I'll have to go Friday. I'm supposed to be comforted by the fact if it were anything serious, the Sister Superior at the Calcutta convent would have called.

A group of us head to a clinic outside Siliguri with Sister Irene, Sister Fiona, and a priest. This clinic is better staffed and better organized than the railway clinic, and it treats not only leprosy patients but those with more general ailments as well.

We make medication bags out of folded paper. The Japanese might impress with their elaborate origami, but Indians contribute a wonderfully practical form of the art. When we have stockpiled the bags, I log medication in a register. Hindus, Christians, and Muslims work side by side.

I notice that when the patients take water with their tablets, no one lets their lips touch the bottle. This is done out of respect for those who will use the bottle after them. That's grace.

❋

Lawrence walks me to the nearby parish center in the evening, to await a call from Jon. In the meantime, I try to reach the convent in Calcutta but can't get through.

Jon manages to get a phone line. He is working in rural Queensland. His crew arrived Monday night in the town and headed out to the field the next morning—only to be delayed when some key machinery broke down. They were forced to turn back. And thank God they did, because heavy rainfall closed many roads due to a cyclone off the coast. Had they forged ahead, they would have been stuck there three days.

As it was, they had to navigate their vehicle through a swollen river five feet deep.

Jon says when I get home, he's going to stem the flow of visitors until we've had time to catch up ourselves. I agree, and suggest one big family dinner early on to say hello. It will then be less urgent to do the rounds of individual visits.

I need to remember to pick up balloons for Sister Agatha, as she's hosting a school picnic.

THE MOTHER TERESA EFFECT

I'm not ready to rock up to church every week, but I make time once or twice a month. I figure it's a start. Her faith fueled her.

GERRY, BATON ROUGE

A friend gave me a book by Mother Teresa. I found the courage to leave an abusive relationship. It was so hard those first six months, and plenty of times I thought of going back to the devil I knew. I stood strong.

MAE, TAMPA

Wednesday, February 12, 1997

It's Ash Wednesday (which starts the forty days of Lent before Easter Sunday). Sister Agatha says I'm too young (at twenty-nine!) to fast today, and she's too old—so in a show of complete logic, we *both* fast.

The day is reasonably warm, and I watch some checkups conducted in the open air. A paramedic runs a knitting needle down the foot of a male patient to gauge his sensitivity. His stock of medications and handheld instruments are wheeled on a small tray that, once upon a time, was used for cocktail glasses and liquor bottles in a fancy Indian home.

Two young girls have been unofficially adopted by the hospital staff, and I smile to watch them playing tag in the front yard. I pause as I notice they're dressed in white—isn't that the color of death here? But I realize it's their First Communion, so white is traditional. They run about beneath the lush wall of orange bougainvillea on the porch.

There is a man who lives on the hospital grounds who has only three teeth, all gnarled and growing in different directions. His prized procession is an old transistor radio, and it seems almost surgically attached. Apparently you should not consider yourself a friend until he allows you to touch it; I'm not sure it even works. I ask a sister what size battery it takes for the next time we head into town.

I walk to the hospital entrance to stretch my legs, and watch as a small boy rides a pony down the road. He's so quietly proud, he might just be a young prince in a parade.

✂

Afternoon brings a house call with Sister Irene. We'll be stopping by the home of a leprosy sufferer who hasn't been seen recently at any of the clinics. He lives with his family of seven in a one-room hut with a dirt floor. Their hospitality is immediate and genuine. And though we have been careful to schedule our visit outside meal times, a bowl of rice appears on the makeshift table. It is offset thoughtfully with a single leaf for decoration. It is likely the only food they have, and yet they offer it to us with happy hearts. I want to decline—how can we eat their only provisions?—but I hesitate, as that would be insulting.

I defer to Sister Irene. She slowly serves us each a spoonful, thanking our hosts without gushing. As we eat, they exhale a little and relax. She compliments the quality of the rice and inquires where they bought it; she plans to recommend the vendor to the hospital's purchasing officer. The father's chest puffs almost indiscernibly. She then serves us each a second and final dollop to reinforce her appreciation. It strikes the perfect note, and it's a lesson in grace to me.

THE MOTHER TERESA EFFECT

People hunger in different ways: for food, sure, but also for companion-
ship, recognition, stability in life. Let's feed those, too.

MAURICE, OKLAHOMA CITY

I helped start a community garden in a food desert. It's taken three
years, but local families are benefiting from affordable, fresh produce.

JOANNA, LAFAYETTE

Thursday, February 13, 1997

I phone the convent in Calcutta straight after Mass.

Auntie was admitted to hospital ten days ago! She has now been home two days. She has had tests, including a scan, amid concerns her osteoporosis is more advanced than first thought.

I head to the railway clinic with Sister Irene, where a wall of arms, legs, and knees are again presented for treatment. Once we are done, I take some photos but run out of film, despite the camera showing that six shots are left. Argh.

Back at the hospital, the house girls, Aisha, Hana, and others, present me with a hair net and hair band, and I'm moved by their generosity of spirit.

I receive an invitation to the wedding of a patient's daughter. Printed invitations would be an unthinkable luxury here. Instead, nuts, flowers, and pieces of fruit are placed on a leaf, and details given verbally.

Speaking of weddings, a former resident of the hospital community is getting married. Her beau, equally poor, asks for a very modest dowry: a bicycle and a simple watch. The head brother promptly fulfills this gracious and agreeable request. If a husband's family is not happy with a dowry, the bride can be persecuted, burned, or beaten.

While chatting at lunch, I'm surprised to learn some Catholic families also post wedding ads. I had always thought of arranged marriages in India as a predominantly Hindu custom. Even when the ads mention a desire that the woman be "convent educated," it's more a social shorthand than a religious issue.

We're joined by a brother from the nearby parish center. He hails from Gujarat state, where he says some local families practice wife-sharing. If an older brother marries first, all his brothers can have sex with his wife until they marry themselves. The woman cannot refuse. A man can sleep only with an older brother's wife, he says, not the spouse of a younger sibling. He adds that decades of selectively aborting females have now resulted in far fewer brides. It's a cruel irony, he sighs: the girls were aborted because they were not valued, and today's brides are now valued for their scarcity.

The staff give me a lovely send-off in the afternoon. They sing songs, and we enjoy a delicious afternoon tea. I feel very spoiled, and we take photos I'll treasure.

I spot this excerpt from a recent newspaper article torn out and pinned to the wall:

Leprosy is grounds for divorce under the Special Marriages Act of 1954 (s. 27 clause g) and the Muslim Marriages Act of 1939 (s. 2, clause VI).

A leprosy sufferer cannot legally drive a vehicle.

Leprosy is legal grounds for sacking.

Unfortunately, the tone of the article reflects the general view of how people regard leprosy sufferers. And, to be fair, it's not only some Indians who feel this way, but many people around the world.

THE MOTHER TERESA EFFECT

In an age of constant distractions, she stayed the course on a single message.   CONNER, AUCKLAND

You can't tell me she woke up every single day with the same vigor as when she first started, but she kept going anyway. Now that I can admire.   BRYANT, SPOKANE

BACK TO CALCUTTA

Friday, February 14, 1997

I wake up feeling seedy. There is a stomach bug going around staff at the hospital.

Ben, one of the religious brothers, is in bed with a torn ligament. I visit to say goodbye and find him determined to recover in time to run the London marathon in April. Lawrence sweetly gives me some film, as I'd run out. They'll leave soon too, and both will profess their final vows to religious life in September.

I almost miss my flight from Bagdogra airport due to a student protest blocking traffic. Rita picks me up in Calcutta. I can't see Auntie Grace today as she is too sick to receive visitors.

I crash around 10:30 P.M.

THE MOTHER TERESA EFFECT

She didn't preach. She lived her faith.   AUSTEN, AUSTIN (REALLY)

I used to throw out so much stuff. I'd donate things too, but I discarded a lot straight to the trash. Now I'm more sensitive to what someone else might use or wear.   TIA, BANGKOK

SAYING GOODBYE
~~~

Saturday, February 15, 1997

I'm determined to sleep in—on sheer principle—but I wake up at 5:30 A.M.

I putter around and then head out for a fifty-minute walk around the pond next door. Everyone is dawdling and doing very outdated stretching exercises. Men are dressed in business attire and wearing slippers; I smile at the incongruity.

Later, Rita and I head to New Market for gifts to take home. She is known for her generosity, but I'm still taken aback when she buys twenty-seven watches! I try to convince her she has already gone above and beyond, but she forges ahead in search of silver-plated milk jugs. The final stop is a store called the Women's Friendly Society, where she selects beautiful linens and dinner napkins.

~~~

I see Auntie Grace in the afternoon, very pale and curled up in her bed. As I walk across her room for this final visit, I tell myself not to cry—but even as I think it, I know it's useless. I have cherished this time with her, and the chance to get to know her more fully. The first time we met, she progressed in my experience from photo to real-life aunt. Now we have enjoyed a more adult relationship, infused with humor and personal stories. I thank her for all she has taught me and share my gratitude for the spiritual doors she has opened, whether cracked ajar in some areas or swung wide open in others. I tell her how much I loved exasperating her. I want to hug her tightly, but her bones are so brittle I fear she might break. She has led a blessed life, she says with a smile, and if God calls her tonight, she is ready.

Grace shares a final experience. She was close to another nun, she says, and the woman found out she had cancer. They would talk for hours, she recalls, their bodies wizened but their minds sharp. "Of course, we believe in Heaven," said Grace to her friend one day. "We have been sisters half a century. But when you get there, will you come back to tell me how beautiful it is?" They laughed about that.

In time, her friend died. Five years later, Grace was getting ready for bed. "I know I wasn't dreaming," she tells me, "because I was fiddling with the button on my nightdress. It was broken, and I reminded myself to give it to a house girl to mend." She turned to her side, and there was her old friend, sitting on her bed. Grace was astounded and quickly made the sign of the cross. "Don't be frightened. It's me," said the friend. "I remembered my promise to you."

Grace found her voice. "What is Heaven like?" she asked. Her friend replied, "It is a thousand times more beautiful and a thousand times more tranquil than we imagined as humans."

Grace says to me, "Child, she was as solid as you are, standing in front of me now." She adds that her friend stayed, smiling, and she could have counted to fifty in the time it took her to fade away.

Ever the teacher, Grace then asks me, "Now, what is the lesson here?"

I say, "Are you kidding? If it takes a nun five years to get to Heaven, how long will it take me?!"

She sighs in resignation and sends her love to all the family, and, with a memory as sharp as ever, recites each one by name. She smiles to remember how naughty my father could be as a boy. I want to ask her more, to draw out one last story to extend our time, but I resist. Her fatigue is showing.

The Sister Superior is out for the day. I cry as I wish the female residents goodbye. One of them, Marie, has written a letter to family friends Joe and Yvonne, who live in Perth, and asks if I would deliver it and take back a violin to have it valued. She remarks casually that she thinks it's a Stradivarius and adds it's okay to keep it. Sure, as if I would.

✂—◯

Back at Rita's apartment, the phone is not working; we walk to her friends' house so I can speak to Jon. He calls a little later than expected, as he'd fallen asleep on the sofa.

On the way back, I see a boy of eight or so on Rita's floor, but something seems a little different about him. I comment that it's nice to see young families in the building. My cousin shifts from one foot to the other and explains he is not "a child of the house" but works for a family in the building; he's one of the millions of children here in servitude. Then it clicks: his clothes, while clean and neat, are not the quality I've seen worn by other children who live here.

After that, we head to a hotel and enjoy dinner and a band. The night wraps up at 3:00 A.M.

THE MOTHER TERESA EFFECT

She found the joy amid such bleakness. If she could find that in the squalor of India, I can look for it a bit more in my own life.

GIL, SACRAMENTO

Some people whine about the world's problems. Others dive into policy and statistics but lose the humanity. She did neither.

SUNITA, KOLKATA

Sunday, February 16, 1997

I'm awake at 7:30 A.M. I do a trial pack while the geezer (hot water system) warms up.

As the morning wears on, a manservant delivers a message to Rita from the family down the road. A second cousin has been corresponding with an Indian gentleman living in London with regard to a potential arranged marriage. He seems nice enough (on the phone, in writing, and by photo) and has good prospects. Equally important, his family presents well, with no immediate red flags sparked by their business interests or social standing (I take this to mean no drunk uncles, premarital pregnancies, or bankruptcy). Everyone is excited to monitor developments.

And everyone *will.*

THE MOTHER TERESA EFFECT

She inspired me to forgive my ex-husband. Well, at least enough so he has a relationship with our kids. I don't know which one of us was more shocked. LUELLA, ATLANTA

As a social worker, I saw genuine need but also a lot of abuse of the system. It started to harden me. I went to a conference and was surprised to see a session on the work of Mother Teresa. It was like a shot in the arm, and I left renewed. CLAIRE, TRENTON

——— # ———

PART V

Back Home

ARRIVING HOME

Monday, February 17, 1997

I board the plane and can barely contain my excitement at seeing Jon again. I'd been hoping for a seat near the front of the coach section, but I'm assigned one of the last rows, as if to fully embrace the smell of the chemical toilets. I write a note to the pilot. It begins, "Dear Sir, greetings from the bowels of your aircraft . . ." I tell him I haven't seen my husband in almost three months, and ask if I could please be at the front of the line in coach when we disembark.

Minutes later, a crew member appears. "Ms. Young, would you like to join us in business class?" she asks. I hadn't been expecting that, but of course I gratefully accept. As I collect my carry-on luggage, I try to ignore the scowls from those around me. The crew is amused that I decline champagne. I explain I don't drink, but as one of them remarks, "This would be a really good time to start."

As the long-haul flight wings its way home, I think of the people I have met and the experiences I've had. Travelers often say, mid-trip, that they reach saturation point at seeing yet another majestic cathedral or stately museum. My time in India offered so much that even amid moments of frustration, it lost none of its sense of theater or ability to captivate, whether visually or spiritually.

After what seems an interminable time, I finally touch down in Perth. I've crossed off the days, checked off lists, and counted down phone calls; now, only one more obstacle remains before I see Jon: Customs. I've been wondering what they'll say about the stash of watches nestled in my bag. I decide that attack is the best defense. I march up to a Customs officer and declare, "Here are twenty-seven watches and a list of who they're for. I have a *big* family."

The official looks at me and says, "Catholic?"

I nod.

"I understand," she says, and waves me through.

OLD ROUTINE, NEW PERSPECTIVE

March 1997

I relish being home again with Jon. Before I left, I had been feeling a little cramped in our two and a half rooms at the boarding house. Now—surprise, surprise—it feels spacious and airy. The bells that sound throughout the day for the students, signaling them variously to lunch or homework or lights out, transport me back to the convent.

We've been apart almost three months, and Jon takes vacation for some much-needed time together. He's a little surprised to see that I've lost ten pounds. This wasn't intended; you simply don't feel like overeating amid striking poverty.

Sorting through mail, I find another reminder of our recent distance: a two-thousand-dollar phone bill. We've never accrued such a high amount for any utility, but we've budgeted for it. It was amusing when the phone company started sending us movie tickets and dinner vouchers to woo us further. We don't drink, smoke, or "do" fine white powder, so I guess we have to spend our money on something.

I had carried Marie's violin home gingerly as part of my hand luggage, and I took it to a local auction house soon after getting back. If it were valuable, I couldn't risk keeping it for any time in the boarding house. It all seemed so unreal—and it was.

The expert at the auction house kindly took the time to point out various features that confirmed it was a good copy in the Stradivarius tradition, but a copy nonetheless. I passed it on to Marie's friends in Perth.

The smallest things take me back to India. I attend a doctor's visit for a checkup. As she puts on gloves, I immediately wonder whose job it is to sort the gloves today at Kalighat.

Later, I'm channel surfing when I see an ad for luxury pet food, brimming with plump chicken, lamb, and fish. I think about how many of the people I had seen in India would give anything to eat it. I continue clicking and come across a documentary. One scene is in a nursing home, and a frail old woman tells the journalist, "If my daughter is watching this, please send a cardigan. I get chilly at night." My heart melts, and I'm instantly back at the convent with all the female residents.

I cringe when I clean out the fridge and toss out tired-looking fruit or vegetables.

MOTHER TERESA'S REPLACEMENT

I'VE BEEN HOME A MATTER of weeks when news breaks that a replacement has been confirmed for Mother Teresa. The sisters at the Missionaries of Charity have voted at their General Chapter Meeting. This is something she has been requesting frequently in recent years. Last time, every vote but one was cast for her to continue her work. That in itself was a *Mother Teresa Effect*. Mother was the only one who had voted for someone else.

Watching the inevitable footage in the news reports evokes the sights and sounds of Kalighat.

Sister Nirmala Joshi has been elected almost unanimously. Her title will be Superior General of the Missionaries of Charity; *Mother* will refer alone to its foundress, guide, and inspiration. Many consider it especially poignant that Sister Nirmala will be taking the helm, as she was born and raised a Hindu, converting to Roman Catholicism later in life.

Given Mother Teresa's frailty and advancing years, I imagine news of this successor is a tremendous relief to her.

MOTHER TERESA'S DEATH

Friday, September 5, 1997

It's been only five days since the world lost Princess Diana to a horrific car crash in a Paris tunnel, and millions around the globe are in mourning for "the People's Princess." Televisions broadcast coverage nonstop, no detail too small to advance her legacy or imbue her aura. We are shown a revolving tapestry of archival footage, from her childhood and shy teenage years, to the wedding that stopped the world and her journey as a mother.

And, just as we catch our breath, comes the news that Mother Teresa has passed away from a heart attack at age eighty-seven, a mere six months after stepping down as the head of the Missionaries of Charity. She was being nursed at Motherhouse in her beloved Calcutta when her final hour came.

(During a hospital stay the year before her death, Mother had complained of insomnia and became more agitated as the night wore on. By coincidence, the Catholic Archbishop of Calcutta, Henry D'Souza, was a patient at the same time. I'm not quite sure how the gist of a conversation moves from "I can't sleep" to "Clearly, you need an exorcism," but the two talked, and the Archbishop summoned a Sicilian priest to conduct an exorcism on Mother Teresa. She was said to have slept peacefully after that.

News of the exorcism broke four years after Mother Teresa's death. After stating the ritual had taken place, Archbishop D'Souza was quoted by media around the world. He then backpedaled in his remarks when controversy flared. Some questioned why an exorcism had been conducted somewhat randomly, without the requisite rigorous inquiry. Others charged that D'Souza had concealed news of the exorcism to prevent it from impeding Mother Teresa's candidacy for sainthood, by possibly being seen to taint her sanctity. Meanwhile, the priest who conducted the ritual, Father Rosario Stroscio, confirmed he had recited prayers of exorcism.)

Once again, the world is reeling from loss.

The prime minister of India immediately declares a national day of mourning. In days to come, this "Saint of the Gutters" will be honored with a full state funeral, an honor normally reserved only for the highest officials. In the meantime, we see images of nuns filing past her body, touching her feet in a sign of respect.

Now, the screens toggle between two stories: the death of Mother Teresa today, and the public funeral of Princess Diana tomorrow, September 6. There is seemingly room for nothing else.

Saturday, September 6, 1997

The shrill ringing of the phone pierces the early-morning quiet. It's a media contact, calling to request a radio interview to discuss my experience in India. The presenter asks my thoughts on the world losing two famous women within days. After the initial shock, it makes sense to me that Mother Teresa would choose to slip away quietly while we're all so focused on someone else.

This is a woman who never sought recognition, nor the prestigious prizes showered on her by her adopted India or by the international community. To be sure, her funeral was a fitting and grand occasion—but as purely a media event, it was eclipsed by the pomp and circumstance of Diana's memorial service.

It's my guess she would have been fine with that.

A commentator sums it up beautifully:

> *Within a week, the world has lost two iconic women.*
>
> *The first was young, beautiful and left behind a personal fortune of sixty million pounds.*
>
> *The other was elderly, her frame hunched, her looks faded.*
>
> *She left behind two saris and a bucket.*

And the legacy of *The Mother Teresa Effect.*

LOSING A ROLE MODEL

April 2006

We're living in Moscow when we learn Grace has passed away at age ninety-four.

The sisters say she remained as sharp as ever until the last twelve months of her life; she then began to fuss over two dolls and relished playing "mommy."

The tears flow, but I'm also happy for her. I know she was ready to be called Home a decade ago. I recall how she came to see me when I was sick, or the stories she told of the family or Mother Teresa. I cherish that time we shared.

As I've written elsewhere, Grace never told me how to live my life; she lived hers, and let me watch.

It's a gift that will stay with me always.

LOOKING BACK

September 2016

Memories are time travel.

It's now twenty years since I took that trip to India, and we are living in the US.

A sound or scent can still transport me back to that dimly lit hospice, to the crowded city streets with cows roaming through traffic, or to the water pump outside the leprosy ward.

Sharing these memories with you has been a privilege and a chance to reflect on my time there.

Mother Teresa now represents a chapter in my life, brief in duration but deep in impact.

My experience didn't play out for me in grand actions. When I got home, I didn't spark a movement, or found a nonprofit, or write an op-ed that made the world sit up.

It washed over me in markedly subtler ways. My own *Mother Teresa Effect* is manifested in small, everyday things.

I learned to bless my bills—yes, those bills that arrive every month. I have a choice to bless them or curse them. The mortgage means we have stability, a roof over our heads, and a warm bed. The cable bill means we can afford entertainment (even if the quality is dubious at times). When an appliance breaks down or a flight is delayed, I try to take stock of these "First World problems" as they surface (some days better than others). I try to remember those who would relish the chance to have these worries. And while I know that food-eating competitions are a harmless tradition of county fairs, I can't watch them for even a moment on the news.

I don't mean to imply that people in the West don't ever struggle or feel distraught by their circumstances. I respect there is very real hardship in every country. I mean simply that developing countries can offer an insight into suffering on a different scale, when you see people living by open sewers. The lucky ones have a roof of rusty corrugated steel, its holes plugged with rags and plastic scraps.

Mother Teresa's face is a shorthand for compassion and a reminder to me to practice gratitude. We can spend so much energy focusing on what we don't have, it's easy to miss everything right in front of us.

My time in India inspired me to look for opportunities to volunteer on vacation and when my husband and I were relocated for work. I have enjoyed stints at an Indonesian orphanage and a Chilean nursing home, among others.

OTHER TAKEAWAYS

I WITNESSED SHEER RESILIENCE in the people on the street, for whom each day is a genuine battle for survival.

I learned the difference between wants and needs, and how we can so easily confuse the two when we live in abundance.

I felt the joy and satisfaction of reaching out of my comfort zone.

I realized we all have the same twenty-four hours in our day. My time in Calcutta inspired me to review how I spend my time, my energy, my dollars, my efforts.

I learned to push past the feeling of hopelessness and the realization that all anyone of us can do is a drop in the ocean. That's true, but it's no reason to do nothing.

I experienced spiritual growth.

I learned a little more patience (still working on that).

I learned to remind myself that when I look at someone, to see the soul inside the shell. Our physical bodies are what we wear this time around, this lifetime. To paraphrase Shakespeare, life is a play, and we are all actors. Given that, is it fair or even logical to envy the one playing the role of king or to pity the pauper?

I learned not to be defeated easily. If those two men at the hospital can overcome a lack of fingers to perform surgery, then I have no right to complain. I often think of them in the face of disappointment.

I recall thinking how the blaring traffic eventually became white noise; I am reminded not to allow spirituality to become its own white noise, but to claim its rightful place in my life.

In recent years, much has been discussed and written of Mother Teresa's crisis of faith. People were shocked to learn that for many years, she felt alone and abandoned. Some felt unsettled to hear this guiding light had harbored doubts about God or her relationship to Him. I think it makes her even more human and genuinely more inspiring that she kept going amid that spiritual darkness. And crucially, her personal doubts never stopped her from seeing the rough diamonds among the destitute.

As a journalist, I've covered events such as the G8 summit, the aftermath of an 8.8 earthquake, and the death of a pope. I've attended White House press briefings and worked with Walter Cronkite. In short, I've had the privilege of meeting people considered leaders in their field, whether in politics, the arts, sports, and beyond.

And yet when I'm asked to nominate the most successful person I've ever encountered, a six-year-old stands out.

This little one appeared at the country hospital each morning at first light. She would be clasping the hand of her four-year-old brother, with her baby sister, perhaps six or eight months old, strapped to her back.

Somehow, she got them up and organized each morning, and presented them for their first meal of the day. As you might imagine, often it was their *only* meal for the day. The nuns had tried to befriend her, but she trusted no one. I can't imagine what her life was like, nor what she had seen or experienced far too early.

Yet she tended to her charges with fierce love and protection.

That is success.

"FIND YOUR OWN CALCUTTA"

I CONSIDER MYSELF VERY fortunate to have traveled to India. That said, of course you don't need to leave home to contribute. There are people in need of our time, companionship, or skills in our own neighborhoods.

Mother Teresa famously said, "Find your own Calcutta." It might mean your local soup kitchen or family shelter. It might mean a senior center with a visitor program, for those who crave company. It might mean helping job-seekers by polishing their résumés.

Maybe you have already found your Calcutta in your own family. Every caregiver tending to an aging spouse or parent, acting as a nurse or advocate, is living *The Mother Teresa Effect*. Every mother or father of a special-needs child reflects her contributions and selflessness every day.

Each time you call a friend going through a hard time, or drop off a meal, or cover for someone at work who has a family emergency, you echo her lessons on kindness and compassion.

When I put out the call for people to contribute their thoughts on her impact, it was startling to see that those who were living a life of service were quick to see it in others but not in themselves. They are the unsung heroes.

Do you recognize *The Mother Teresa Effect* in you?

— // —

THINKING OF TRAVELING TO INDIA?

BEFORE YOU GO

Visit your doctor or a traveler's medical clinic to ensure you have the right shots: typhoid, hepatitis (a series of vaccinations), and tetanus are the main ones. You will also get advice on antimalarials and updates on any other current health risks.

It's tempting to stay in the low-cost rooms on Sudder Street, but though your budget might be tight, spring a bit more for the best accommodation you can afford. Many volunteers told me that the dormitories, while a good place to meet people, became overwhelming, and petty theft or permanent "borrowing" of things became irritating. After a day at work, you'll welcome a bit of privacy.

Pack modest clothes, toiletries, and prescriptions for any medication you take, along with the medication itself in its original packaging. Likewise, include a prescription for your glasses or contact lenses.

If you plan to take your phone, check with your provider about roaming charges. If they're too expensive, you might be able to use your phone simply as a camera. Keep it on "airplane mode" to ensure calls can't be made or received, and to avoid draining the battery. Local SIM cards can be difficult for foreigners to buy.

Pack a journal! Yes, a journal. A real-life, paper diary. Technology changes, emails get lost, and computer systems freeze. Have a backup.

Search online for traveler reviews of accommodations and other tips.

As I did, many people think they need to preregister to volunteer before they arrive. This isn't necessary.

I completely understand the lure of volunteering in Kolkata! But India is a huge country, and your help is needed in many other places—not only in big cities. Consider another location instead of Kolkata or in addition to it.

ONCE THERE

Visit Motherhouse at 54A AJC Bose Road to register as a volunteer and to designate the Missionaries of Charity's home(s) where you'd like to be based. You'll need to show your passport.

When I was there, photos were permitted at some facilities; I understand this is no longer a given. Please respect requests not to film or take photos. And please, oh please, no selfies in front of terminally ill people (yes, it's happened).

As with any travel, stay mindful of your surroundings.

Beware of scams, especially outside tourist attractions, temples, or Motherhouse itself by people claiming to be guides.

Volunteering can be physically and emotionally draining. Be gentle to yourself on your time off. Discover wonderful places to eat, check out dance clubs, and soak up the history and museums. Perhaps most of all, wander beyond the expat bubble to meet locals.

BACK HOME

Resist the urge to begin every sentence with "In India . . ."

Give yourself a little time to decompress.

And keep that journal going, as insights and lessons will keep surfacing long after you unpack.

ACKNOWLEDGMENTS

THE IDEA FOR *The Mother Teresa Effect* came when I was leafing through a box of photos and letters of my time in India. I reflected on the cast of characters I had met in my time there, and how I had witnessed the best and worst of human nature. Three weeks later, the first draft was staring back at me onscreen.

Support Team
My thanks to Holly Young for her unrelenting support and thought-provoking questions, and for reading and brainstorming at all hours and across all time zones. Thanks also to Charmaine Lobo (loboluxe.com; intrepidallergymum.com) to whom this book is dedicated and for posing just the right question at just the right time, when I wanted to give up and flee to Kazakhstan under an assumed name.

Likewise my appreciation to Christina Street (née Riviere) for combing through the manuscript to provide thoughtful feedback as to balance and content; to Megan Cammilleri (née Pegrum) for lending perspective and calming good humor to harried moments; to Grace Mattioli (gracemattioli.com) for sharing her publishing knowledge, which is both considered and considerable; to Ihaan Adriansz and Tania D'Ercole for their thoughtful and measured feedback, which both boosts me and challenges me to think through a different prism.

Most of all, my loving thanks to Jon, whose name means "Gift from God" and who is my gift. Writing this book spilled repeatedly into our shared time. His patience, endless cups of English breakfast tea, and incredible support is a lesson in loving grace to me. Your laughter is my shorthand for happiness. One of my favorite sounds is your key in the door.

Editorial Team
To Theresa Duran (duraneditorial.com) for her humor, allergy to error, and a trained eye that could just as well have been deployed in espionage; to Amy Apel (amyapel.com) for her beautifully crisp index and for being so easy to work with.

Design Team
To Lynn Bell of Monroe Street Studios (monroest.com) for her delightful interior, which infuses whimsy and substance, and for her creative, inspired cover design; to Ciara Flood (ciaraflood.co.uk) for her elegant cover illustration, which captures the essence of an icon with grace and wit; to the dynamic team at Light Story (lightstory.com.au) for its creative cover photography and artistic insight; and to Val Gaino (buenaondaimports.com) for her valuable input during early-stage development.

Anecdotes and Cultural Consultants
My thanks to all those who contributed their thoughts and experiences. Special thanks to Jo Gillausseyn, Soledad Tanner (soledadtanner.com), and Kathy Kest. Also, I am indebted to Rashmi Singhvi and Joseph Ponnoly for their cultural insight. Further thanks to Jacquie Mackay of ABC radio, Australia (www.abc.net.au/capricornia/programs/capricornia_breakfast/).

Legal Counsel
To Alan Korn (alankorn.com) for his sound legal advice.

Acknowledgment of Trademarks and Copyright
The author and Parasol Press LLC thank the following artists and manufacturers, and acknowledge their rightful ownership of their corresponding trademarks: AmeriCares (americares.org); Bayerische Motoren Werke AG (aka BMW, bmwusa.com); The Nobel Foundation (nobelprize.org);

The Nun Bun/Bongo Java (bongojava.com); Peanuts Worldwide LLC and Charles M. Schulz, creator of the *Peanuts* comic strip (peanuts.com); Polaroid film (polaroid.com); TACA Airlines (tacaairlines.ca).

Charitable Organizations
Various charities and websites are mentioned throughout this book and are provided in good faith. Readers are urged to conduct their own inquiries and to be satisfied with same before considering any donation or other support. Parasol Press LLC and the author are not responsible for any party's experience with any given charity or entity. Thank you for your understanding.

Further Reading and Book Club Discussion Sheets
A list of resources is kept on my website at motherteresaeffect.net (which may redirect to my main site, aliciayoung.net).

———*//*———

SELECT BIBLIOGRAPHY

INTRODUCTION

Sister Act (film). Directed by Emile Ardolino; screenplay by Joseph Howard. Touchstone Pictures / Touchwood Partners, 1992.

Teresa, Mother. Nobel Lecture (Oslo, Norway, December 11, 1979). http://www.nobelprize.org/nobel_prizes/peace/laureates/1979/teresa-lecture.html.

MOTHER TERESA: HER LIFE IN BRIEF

Books

Langford, Joseph. *Mother Teresa's Secret Fire: The Encounter That Changed Her Life, and How It Can Transform Your Own*. Huntington, IN: Our Sunday Visitor, 2008.

Teresa, Mother. *Come Be My Light: The Private Writings of the Saint of Calcutta*. Edited and with commentary by Brian Kolodiejchuk, MC. New York: Doubleday Religion / The Mother Teresa Center, 2007.

————. *In My Own Words, 1910–1997*. Compiled by José Luis Gonzáles-Balado. New York: Gramercy Books, 1996.

————. *The Joy in Loving: A Guide to Daily Living with Mother Teresa*. Compiled by Jaya Chaliha and Edward Le Joly. New York: Penguin Compass, 1996.

———. *No Greater Love.* Foreword by Thomas Moore. Novato, CA: New World Library, 1989.

———. *A Simple Path.* Compiled by Lucinda Vardey. New York: Ballantine Books, 1995.

———. *Where There Is Love, There Is God: Her Path to Closer Union with God and Greater Love for Others.* Edited and with commentary by Brian Kolodiejchuk, MC. New York: Doubleday Religion / The Mother Teresa Center, 2010.

Online Biographies

Biography.com. "Mother Teresa of Calcutta." http://www.biography.com/people/mother-teresa-9504160#synopsis.

Nobel Foundation. "Mother Teresa." http://www.nobelprize.org/nobel_prizes/peace/laureates/1979/teresa-bio.html.

Vatican Information Service. "Mother Teresa of Calcutta." http://www.vatican.va/news_services/liturgy/saints/ns_lit_doc_20031019_madre-teresa_en.html.

PART II: KALIGHAT

Muggeridge, Malcolm. *Something Beautiful for God.* New York: Harper & Row, 1971.

PART III: CHRISTMAS AND NEW YEAR

City of Joy (film). Directed by Roland Joffé; screenplay by Mark Medoff. Allied Filmmakers / Lightmotive / Pricel, 1992.

Lapierre, Dominique. *City of Joy.* Translated from the French by Kathryn Spink. New York: Doubleday, 1985.

"Kidnapped 'Nun Bun' Resurfaces in Seattle." Boing Boing, March 15, 2007. http://boingboing.net/2007/03/15/kidnapped-nun-bun-re.html.

"Mother Teresa Not Amused by Nun Bun." *Seattle Times*, May 23, 1997. http://community.seattletimes.nwsource.com/archive/?date=19970523&slug=2540738.

PART V: BACK HOME

"Did Mother Teresa Need an Exorcist?" *Time*, September 5, 2001 .http://content.time.com/time/world/article/0,8599,173791,00 .html.

"Exorcism Performed on Mother Teresa." BBC News, September 6, 2001. http://news.bbc.co.uk/2/hi/south_asia/1529093.stm.

"That One Time Mother Teresa Was Given an Exorcism." Today I Found Out, August 25, 2015. http://www.todayifoundout.com/index.php/2015/08/one-time-mother-teresa-given-exorcism/

———— // ————

ABOUT THE AUTHOR

⮑∽∾⮐

ALICIA YOUNG IS A US-based Australian television journalist with more than fifteen years' experience in local, national, and international news. Her passion for current events propelled her to Russia (where she presented the news in Moscow), the US, UK, and Europe. She has contributed to newsrooms around the world as an anchor, medical reporter, and international correspondent. She has worked with Walter Cronkite, filed live reports from Rome on the death of Pope John Paul II, covered various presidential elections/inaugurations, and reported on the aftermath of the magnitude 8.8 earthquake that rocked Chile in 2010.

Prior to journalism, Alicia was a social worker and crisis counselor in the areas of child protection and mental health.

Alicia was once told off by Mother Teresa for not having children (she forgot) and has volunteered at a hospice and leprosy hospital in India. Outside work, Alicia handles parasols and power tools with equal ease (not really, but she helpfully holds the flashlight while her better half fixes things around the house).

Learn more at aliciayoung.net and motherteresaeffect.net.

———※———

SPEAKING ENGAGEMENTS

Alicia is a dynamic and engaging speaker, drawing on her global travel and background in television and radio news to weave stories around a range of topics. She welcomes inquiries for speaking opportunities throughout the US and around the world.

ORDERING THE BOOK/BULK PURCHASES

The Mother Teresa Effect is available as both an ebook and soft-cover on Amazon. It is offered in a regular version and a family edition. For bulk print orders, please contact Parasol Press LLC. Places of worship, community groups, and organizations can buy in bulk to present as gifts to their members or conference attendees. Copies can also be purchased wholesale in order to raise both funds and awareness.

CONTACT

Parasol Press LLC
PO Box 980456, Houston, TX 77098-0456
info@parasolpress.net

A REQUEST

I hope you have enjoyed sharing my journey to India. If you have a moment, I'd very much appreciate a quick Amazon review. You can find a link on my website, aliciayoung.net. And I'd love to hear about your own *Mother Teresa Effect!*

Thank you.

Alicia
@AliciaWriter

———— // ————

THE 12 STAMPS PROJECT
*(Because we're more logged on than ever,
but less connected)*

~~~❦~~~

THE 12 STAMPS PROJECT IS a fun initiative to tap the power of the handwritten word and boost literacy. It's vital in a digital age, when it seems we're surgically attached to our screens. Someone in your life needs to hear from you; rediscover the impact of a card or letter on others.

Our premise is simple but potent: buy twelve stamps and commit to sending twelve notes this year. Send a note to thank someone who helped you out, whether yesterday or in your childhood. Let them know what their support meant to you. Imagine your words of comfort to someone who is navigating change, or who feels a little isolated, lonely, or stressed with job hunting. Share a joke, a quirky observation, or a passionate opinion. Do you recall a special letter or note that boosted or encouraged you? Maybe it celebrated a big milestone or a small act that still resonates for you. Share your ideas at @12stamps—we'd love to hear from you!

How do I get started?
All it takes is the stamps, paper, and a willingness to have an impact. Some people start a small group at work, their after-school club, or sorority, while others distribute the stamps among family members.

An easy way to make a child feel important? Send them mail! Write to your niece, nephew, or teen cousin. Tell them that you've noticed how well they share, or the confident reader they've become, or how much they'll love college. We've seen everyone from first graders to professional athletes swell with pride. And a child or teen who receives a letter is more likely to write one; this is a powerful life skill for everything from a thank-you note to a job application.

Alicia
@12Stamps

DONATIONS

THE MISSIONARIES OF Charity are active in more than 120 countries in myriad languages, so I suggest that you conduct a local search if you wish to donate.

Please also consider supporting the vital work of Jesu Ashram (jesuashram.in).

For a directory of Indian charities, please visit GlobalGiving (globalgiving.org).

INDEX

A

Acha (expression), 38, 97
Adoption of orphans, 51
Agatha, Sister, 105, 115, 117
AmeriCares (charity), 72
Amnesty International, 54
Amputation, 97–98
Anglo-Indians, 10, 30, 63, 66
Animal sacrifice, 40
Arranged marriages, 22, 47–48, 120, 125

B

Barnabus, Saint, 79–80
Basanti, India (town), 70–71
Bathing, 23, 30, 36, 41, 42, 95
Begging and beggars, 18, 20, 34, 75, 102, 111. *See also* Homeless people
Blackouts, 98, 99, 108, 112
Blessings, counting one's, 134
Bojaxhiu, Gonxha Agnes, 16. *See also* Mother Teresa
Bollywood movies, 77–79
Bras, 103

C

Calcutta, India (city). *See also* India
crowdedness of, 23–25
lodgings, 20, 139
noise, 27, 66, 69, 77, 135
scams, 75
traffic conditions, 18
weather, 18, 39, 48
Young family origins in, 11
Call to religious service, 16, 74, 87, 89, 113–114
Caste system, 46, 47, 48
Charitable giving, 31, 39, 40, 53, 58, 77, 101, 109
Children. *See also* Indian children
Mother Teresa Effect upon, 9–10, 22, 28, 47, 53, 60
orphans and orphanages, 20, 42, 47, 51, 58, 59–60, 68, 111
Christmas, 53, 56, 60–61, 62
City of Joy (film and book), 58–59
Community, 104, 107
Compassion, 26, 31, 37, 108, 134, 137
Contraception, 57, 79

Convent life
    abusive servants, 66, 76
    funerals, 72
    lack of privacy, 61
    leisure activities, 68, 89
    living conditions, 29–30
    residents and grounds, 49–50,
        53–54, 64–65
    silent retreats, 74
Cremation, 18, 52, 84

D
Dalai Lama, 22
Daughters Rising (charity), 53
Death
    of Auntie Grace, 133
    at convent, 72
    "good death," 35, 52
    at Kalighat, 35, 52, 67
    of Mother Teresa, 131–132
    Parsi customs, 112
    white as color of, 21, 117
    Young family attitudes about, 11
Diana, Princess of Wales, 131–132
Diapers, 44, 59
Disabled people, 45
Domestic staff, 18–19, 41, 66, 76,
    124
Donations. See also Begging and
    beggars
    of goods, 41, 62, 67, 71, 73, 82,
        84, 122
    of money, 39, 40, 53, 58, 77, 101,
        109, 151
Dowries, 59, 119
D'Souza, Henry, Archbishop, 131
Dulcie, Auntie, 67

E
Enneagrams, 113–114
Exorcism, 131

F
Faith, living one's, 87, 117, 122, 124
Fax communication, 39, 79, 86, 98,
    113, 114
Finding your own Calcutta, 137
"First World problems," 134
Food
    begging for, 34
    donations of, 20, 40, 45, 73
    hunger and malnutrition, 34, 65,
        94, 107, 119
    Indian food, 30, 38
    in Indian hospitality, 19, 21–22,
        118
    provided by charities, 43
    waste of, 31, 113, 134

G
God
    Auntie Grace's faith in, 74, 87
    calling to religious service, 16, 74,
        87, 89, 113–114
    Mother Teresa's faith in, 20, 26,
        135
Gold, 21
Goodwill (charity), 62
Grace, Auntie. See also Convent life
    Alicia's goodbye with, 122–123
    Alicia's relationship with, 29, 49,
        83, 89–90
    death, 133
    habit of, 10
    health, 85–86, 96, 116

Grace, Auntie (*continued*)
  relationship with other nuns, 64
  religious calling, 87–88
  silent retreat, 74
  work with Mother Teresa, 20, 72,
    111
Gracious gestures, 11, 30, 51, 64,
    67, 81, 116, 118. *See also*
    Mother Teresa Effect
Gratitude, 62, 134

H

Habit (religious garb), 10, 35, 71, 89
Hindus and Hinduism, 18, 20, 21,
    61, 116, 120
HIV/AIDS, 99
Home for the Dying Destitute. *See*
    Kalighat
Homeless people
  begging and beggars, 18, 20, 34,
    75, 102, 111
  mobile clinics for, 106–107
  Mother Teresa Effect and, 45, 69,
    79, 82–83, 114
  resilience of, 135
Hospitals, 70, 85–86, 95, 102
Howra, India (city), 58–59
Hunger and malnutrition, 34, 65,
    94, 107, 119

I

Immunizations, 18, 94
India. *See also* Calcutta
  clothing, 24, 35, 45, 48, 71, 132
  food, 19, 30, 36, 38, 43, 65
  hospitality, 18–19, 65, 70, 118
  inefficiency, 114

jewelry, 19, 21, 69
manner of walking, 19
mannerisms, 38, 54
markets, 70, 105, 115
marriage customs, 21–22, 46–48,
    69, 76, 119–120, 125
medical care and hospitals, 41, 67,
    70, 83, 95, 97, 102, 106–107
movie theaters, 77–78
noise, 27, 66, 69, 77, 135
traveling to, 139–140
urban conditions, 59, 69, 70, 134
voluntarism of Indian people, 13
weddings, 21–22, 119
women's status, 46, 49, 120
Indian children. *See also* Orphans
    and orphanages
  aborting of females, 120
  as caregivers, 109–110, 136
  at leprosy ward, 102, 109
  maiming of, 75
  as servants, 124
  street children, 23, 38, 42–43,
    75, 107
  stunted growth of, 102

J

Jewelry, 19, 21, 69
Jon (Alicia's husband)
  communications with Alicia, 30,
    67, 79, 100, 105, 108–109,
    116–117
  early relationship with Alicia, 11
  reunion with Alicia, 129
  support for Alicia's volunteer
    work, 11–12, 79
  visit to India, 18–19, 22, 25

worry that Alicia will become a
nun, 12, 89
Journal writing, 139–140
Joy, 41, 81, 89, 111, 112, 124, 135

K

Kali (goddess), 40
Kalighat (Home for the Dying
Destitute)
Alicia's choice of, 28
Christmas, 53, 56, 60–61, 62
condition of patients, 34–35, 63,
83
death rituals, 62, 84
as divinely lit, 39–40, 61
emotional experience of volunteers, 44, 67, 90–91
food, 36
glut of volunteers at, 60, 71
Kolkata. *See* Calcutta
Kurseong, India (town), 110–111

L

Language differences, 35, 43, 81
Lapierre, Dominique, 58–59
Laundry, 41, 62
Leprosy and lepers
shoes as important to, 115
stigma of leprosy, 12, 120
susceptibility to leprosy, 94
symptoms of leprosy, 97, 102
Leprosy ward
Alicia's arrival at, 94–96
Alicia's choice to work in, 12
amputations, 97–98
condition of patients, 101, 117
volunteer duties, 95, 97, 99–100

Letter writing, 37, 54, 79, 88, 99,
108, 150
Locks of Love (charity), 82
Loneliness, 48, 52, 54, 137, 150

M

Macauley, Bob, 72–73
Maggot therapy, 101
Mail service, 38, 46, 69, 76
Malaria, 16, 30, 34, 83, 139
Malnutrition and hunger, 34, 65,
94, 107, 119
Manual labor and relating to the
poor, 36, 41
Marriage customs, 21–22, 46–48,
69, 76, 119–120, 125
Massage, 45
Medical care, standards of
in Basanti, 70
at the convent, 83
at Kalighat, 41, 67
at the leprosy ward, 97–98, 102
in the mobile clinic, 106–107
Missionaries of Charity (religious
order). *See also* Kalighat (Home
for the Dying Destitute);
Mother Teresa; Motherhouse
Brothers of, 35, 62, 121
donations to, 44, 51, 151
founding of, 16, 20–21
glut of volunteers, 12
laundry, 41
medical care, 41, 67
Mother Teresa's successor, 130
orphanages, 28, 47, 51, 59–60,
73, 79
power of touch at, 43

Missionaries of Charity (*continued*)
  volunteers tasks, 71, 81
  vow of poverty, 71–72
Mosquito repellent, 80
Mother Teresa
  on abortion and contraception,
    51, 57
  Alicia's audience with, 56–57
  Alicia's correspondence with, 12
  compassion of, 26, 134
  Dalai Lama on, 22
  death, 131–132
  early life, 15–16
  faith in God, 20, 26, 135
  health, 28, 56, 61
  letters from, 12, 26
  on manual labor, 36, 41
  Nobel Prize, 9
  "Nun Bun," 73–74
  on sharing, 9
  successor to, 130
  travel, 16, 72–73
  usefulness of fame, 88
Mother Teresa Effect
  about, 13
  appreciating coworkers, 109
  attending church, 79, 117
  celebrating achievements of oth-
    ers, 108
  upon children, 9–10, 53, 60
  committing random acts of kind-
    ness, 81, 90
  contributing money, 31, 39, 40,
    53, 58, 77, 101, 109
  detaching morality from poverty, 44
  donating goods, 62, 71, 82, 84, 122

easing loneliness, 48, 52, 54
finding joy in serving others, 112,
  124
as finding your own Calcutta, 137
focusing on achieving goals, 91,
  95, 99, 106, 111, 121
forgiving others and self, 68, 84,
  125
foster parenting, 68
giving second chances, 100
giving to others, 51, 63, 66, 67,
  86
helping neighbors, 40, 74, 75, 96,
  101, 111
including others, 80
leaving abusive relationships, 117
letting go of jealousy, 90
listening to others, 44, 66, 77
living one's faith, 122
loving others, 47
making career choices, 100
making gracious gestures, 51, 64,
  67, 81
making hiring decisions, 45, 115
mentoring others, 37, 64, 73
overcoming cynicism, 125
parenting and family, 75, 79, 91
praying, 60, 80, 88, 96, 106
reducing gossip, 112
serving homeless people, 45, 69,
  79, 82–83, 114
serving others as a privilege, 110
strengthening community, 104,
  119
treating others with compassion,
  22, 31, 37, 108, 137

treating others with respect and
dignity, 28, 62, 69, 81

treating people equally, 113

volunteering, 42, 48, 54, 62, 65,
68, 71, 73, 110, 115

not wasting food, 113

wearing makeup, 95

welcoming newcomers, 63, 64

Mother Teresa's Center for the
Homeless (Mauritius), 31

Motherhouse. *See also* Missionaries
of Charity

Christmas, 61

European visitors, 65

Mass, 58

Mother Teresa's presence at, 28,
51, 56, 61, 131

volunteers at, 26, 27–28, 140

Muggeridge, Malcolm, 39–40, 61

N

Nabo Jibon House (orphanage), 42

New Zealanders, 53

Nirmal Hriday. *See* Kalighat (Home
for the Dying Destitute)

Nirmala Joshi, Sister, 130

Nirmala Shishu Bhavan orphanage,
28, 51, 59–60, 73, 79

Nobel Prize, 9

Noise, 27, 66, 69, 77, 135

Nonjudgment, 26

Novices, 15, 35, 56

"Nun Bun," 73–74

Nuns. *See* Convent life; Grace,
Auntie; Missionaries of Charity;
Mother Teresa

O

Orphans and orphanages, 20, 42, 47,
51, 58, 59–60, 68, 111. *See also*
Indian children; Shishu Bhavan

P

Phone book, 46

The poor

compassion for, 31

hospitality of, 118

manual labor and relating to, 36,
41, 72

Mother Teresa's calling to work
with, 15–16

Post office, 38, 46, 69, 76

Poverty

detaching morality from, 44

giving up children due to, 59

in Third World, 134

vows of, 16, 41, 72, 132

Power outages, 98, 99, 108, 112

Privacy, 23–25, 37, 61, 63, 139

R

Rita (Alicia's aunt)

as guide to Indian society, 45–46,
63, 69, 77–78, 122

lifestyle, 18–19, 124–125

S

Salwar kameez (garment), 48

Saris, 24, 35, 45, 71, 132

Servants, 18–19, 41, 66, 76, 124

Sex trafficking, 49, 53

Sharing, 47, 82

Shishu Bhavan orphanage, 28, 51, 59–60, 73, 79. *See also* Indian children; Orphans and orphanages
Sight into Sound (charity), 110
Simplicity, 29, 36, 44
Sister Act (film), 10, 89
Skin color and social status, 24, 46, 49–50
Spirituality, 56, 61, 74, 114, 123, 135
Sponsorship requests, 107
Success, standards for, 136

T
Tea, 36, 58, 87
Teresa, Mother. *See* Mother Teresa
Thérèse of Lisieux, Saint, 16
30-Hour Famine (charity), 65
Tim Tams (cookies), 82
Touch, power of, 43, 114
Traffic conditions, 18, 23–25
Traveling to India, 139–140
12 Stamps Project, 150

V
Vaccinations, 18, 94, 139
Vatican, 16
Volunteers and volunteering. *See also* Kalighat; Leprosy ward
Alicia's ongoing volunteering, 134
emotional experience of, 31, 42, 44, 67, 90–91
as finding your own Calcutta, 137
Mother Teresa Effect, 42, 48, 54, 62, 65, 68, 71, 73, 110, 115

opportunities in India, 140
in Young family, 10–11

W
Walking in India, 19, 100–101, 103–104
Wasting time, 135
Weather in Calcutta, 18, 39, 48
Wedding ads, 46–47, 120
Western volunteers in India, 13, 27
Wife sharing, 120
Women in India, 46, 49, 120

Y
Young, Alicia
Anglo-Indian Catholic background, 10–11
arrival in India, 18–22
audience with Mother Teresa, 56–58
Christmas in India, 60–63
convent life, 29–30, 38, 41, 49–54, 64–66, 68, 72, 74, 86–90
departure from India, 121–125
dress-up in habit, 89
early interest in Mother Teresa, 9
first impressions of Calcutta, 23–25, 39–40, 46
first impressions of Kalighat, 34–37
friends and family at home, 88–89, 108
illnesses, 52–53, 83–84
interviews with the media, 86, 105, 132

lessons learned from volunteering,
    13–14, 134, 135–136
planning for trip to India, 11–13
prayers, 38, 42, 103
reflections on experience in India,
    133–136
registration as a volunteer, 27–28
relationship with Auntie Grace, 29,
    49, 83, 89–90, 122–123, 133
return to Australia, 128–130
reunion with Jon, 129
separation from Jon, 25, 102, 105,
    112, 128
spirituality, 135
volunteer tasks at Kalighat, 13,
    36–37, 41, 48–49
volunteer tasks at leprosy ward, 95,
    97, 99–101, 106–107, 116
volunteering after India trip, 134

www.ingramcontent.com/pod-product-compliance
Lightning Source LLC
Chambersburg PA
CBHW031623040426
42452CB00007B/642